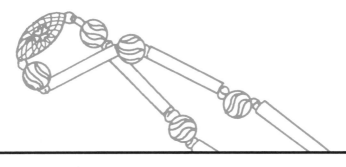

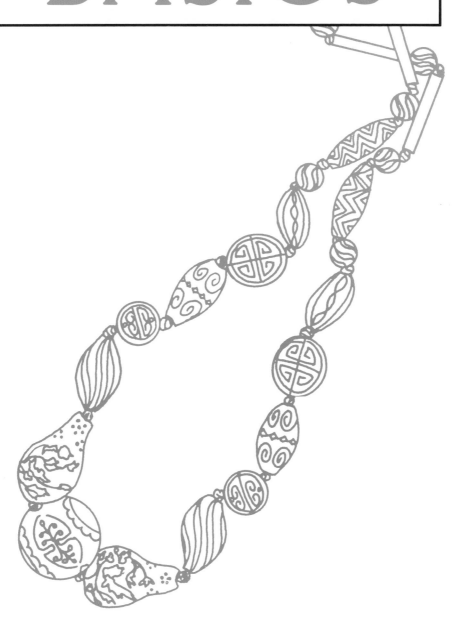

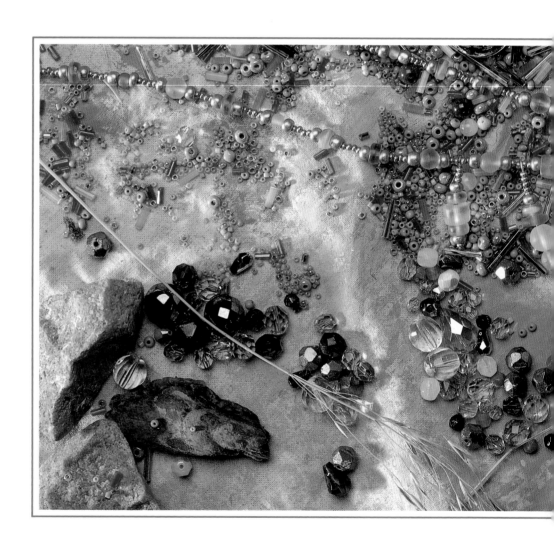

Beadwork
B·A·S·I·C·S

Ann Benson

A Sterling/Chapelle Book
Sterling Publishing Co., Inc. New York

For Chapelle
Owner
Jo Packham

Staff
Sandra Anderson, Malissa Boatwright, Trice Boerens, Rebecca Christensen, Holly Fuller, Cherie Hanson, Holly Hollingsworth, Susan Jorgensen, Susan Laws, Lorin May, Tammy Perkins, Jamie C. Pierce, Leslie Ridenour, Edie Stockstill, and Nancy Whitley

Book Design and Editorial: Petersen Communications

Photographers: Ryne Hazen and Kevin Dilley

The photographs featured in this book were taken at the homes of Edie Stockstill and Jo Packham

Special thanks go to Edie Stockstill and Jamie C. Pierce

Library of Congress Cataloging-in-Publication Data

Benson, Ann.
    Beadwork basics / by Ann Benson.
        p.   cm.
    "A Sterling/Chapelle book."
    Includes index.
    ISBN 0-8069-0877-7
    1. Beadwork.   2. Jewelry making.   I. Title.   II. Title: Beadweaving basics.
TT860.B46   1994   94-25633
745.58'2—dc20   CIP

10 9 8 7 6 5 4 3 2 1

A Sterling/Chapelle Book

Published by Sterling Publishing Company, Inc.
387 Park Avenue South, New York, N.Y. 10016
©1994 by Chapelle Ltd.
Distributed in Canada by Sterling Publishing
c/o Canadian Manda Group, P.O. Box 920, Station U
Toronto, Ontario, Canada M8Z 5P9
Distributed in Great Britain and Europe by Cassell PLC
Villiers House, 41/47 Strand, London WC2N 5JE, England
Distributed in Australia by Capricorn Link Ltd.
P.O. Box 665, Lane Cove, NSW 2066
Printed and bound in Hong Kong
All rights reserved

Sterling ISBN 0-8069-0877-7

To Jane Gallagher Ritson

The Last (and Best)

of the Leprechauns

Ann Benson is a well-known designer specializing in beaded jewelry and needlearts. In addition to designing many craft and needleart publications, she also co-authors several board games.

When Ann is not designing her beautiful beaded creations, she enjoys choral singing, bicycling and interior carpentry.

Miss Benson resides with her family in Amherst, Massachusetts.

Contents

Large Glass Beads

It's no wonder we use more glass beads than any other kind; there are so many available that it is nearly impossible to catalog them all.

Glass beads are either molded or hand-blown. Molded beads are readily available and can be made in almost any color of glass; you might find thirty colors of round glass beads (druks) available in just one bead store on any given day. Affordability is rarely a problem when buying molded glass beads; your biggest problem will be deciding what you want, since the choices are so numerous.

Hand-blown glass beads can be exquisitely beautiful. Although there are some standards of style and shape that are relatively easy to locate, each bead is the individual work of one particular artist, and therefore unique and precious. Naturally, this is reflected in the price; it is not unusual to pay several dollars for only one very fine bead. But that one gorgeous bead can be the centerpiece for a very fine piece of jewelry, and you'll forget the price after the first compliment.

Bone Beads

Like wood and stone beads, those made of bone have a wonderful natural luster. Because it is quite a durable substance, beads made from bone have lasted millennia; indeed, some of the oldest known objects identifiable as beads are made of bone.

There is a wide range of coloration, especially in those made of horn or tusk. Many bone beads are startlingly white, and others nearly black; there are many rich hues of brown in between. Bone beads are frequently carved.

Synthetic bone beads are a good substitute if you are not concerned with authenticity.

Rough Ceramic Beads

The materials used to create rough ceramic beads are not unlike those used in making decorated ceramic beads; the real difference in their appearance lies in the way the surfaces are treated.

While some "rough" ceramic beads are actually glazed, the glazes themselves are grainy and rough after firing, and the resulting appearance is that of a colored but unglazed bead. While most are molded, some are extruded like pasta. These beads tend to have soft, natural colors like the materials from which they are made, but some variety can be introduced by adding dyes to the clay before forming the beads.

Synthetic Clay Beads

Synthetic clay is truly a modern wonder. With Fimo™, Sculpey™, Cernit™ and Formello™, we can make any bead we want to make at any time we want to make it. As a child, I would sit for hours in what was then called a Baby Butler (a table on wheels with me securely enclosed in a seat in the center of it) and make tiny little swans from modeling clay. Now I have tiny little swan earrings, made from tiny little swan beads, made from tiny little amounts of Fimo. I even made some for my mother.

This activity is now considered artistically correct, even for those of us who suffer from adulthood. There are many fine instructional books on the subject of making clay beads; choose the one that suits you best, buy some clay, and make whatever you want!

Metal Beads

The price of a metal bead is largely determined by its precious metal content. Sterling silver beads can be very pricey, while their plated counterparts are remarkably affordable. Gold-filled or gold-plated beads can actually be purchased for less than the average beader's weekly income; however, few people can afford to buy enough 14-carat gold beads at one time to make anything of significance.

But take heart! There are a tremendous number of styles and sizes available in surface-washed base metal beads, which can be breathtakingly beautiful. And unless you're intent on impressing someone, the best-kept secret in many jewelry boxes is plastic beads washed with a precious metal finish. They are readily available, lightweight, inexpensive and great-looking. Much more rewarding than buying one gold bead a year and hoping you'll live long enough to finish your necklace!

Faux Pearls

False pearls can be dyed to just about any color imaginable, and are available in a wide range of shapes and sizes. Some are coated plastic, while others are pearlized glass.

In either case, the imitations can be quite good; it is sometimes necessary to use the trick of rubbing the pearl against your teeth to determine if it is the real thing. If a pearl is genuine, the microscopic scales of nacre (the lustrous substance on its surface) will grate against your teeth, causing a very unpleasant sensation. It might be a better idea just to wonder.

Shell Beads

Shells have been used in many cultures as a medium of exchange; it is no surprise that some people still impart this value to shells, for they can be very precious and beautiful indeed. The "beads" made from shells are seldom ordinary in shape or size or coloration; often they are strange and irregular, and therefore very interesting. More often, shells will be made into chips or dangles which may be combined with other beads made of different substances.

Plastic Beads

Better beading through chemistry! Some of the most exciting beads available are made of plastic. They can be pale and translucent or wildly colorful, crisp-edged or softly molded into gentle flowing shapes. The variation of beads available in plastic is nearly endless.

Plastic offers several advantages to the serious beadworker, not the least of which is its relative affordability. Plastic imitations of semi-precious beads look great for a fraction of the cost of the genuine article. These beads are lightweight and consistently strong, and since plastic is almost always fabricated by molding, the holes are uniform. This makes plastic an ideal candidate for use on heavier-weight cords or multiple strand cords.

Wood Beads

Like other beads made from naturally occurring substances, wooden beads have a special kind of beauty. They mix well with just about anything; they are lightweight, relatively inexpensive and widely available.

Many varieties of wood are used to make beads; each is unique depending on its grain and finish. Unlacquered wood beads can be soaked in vanilla or fragrant oils and worn as perfume. Beads made from natural sandalwood have the familiar and enticing odor which is often extracted from the wood and used for other purposes.

These days, wood beads are often manufactured in factories with huge lathes, grinders, tumblers and sanders. But anyone with even the simplest woodworking tools can make a fine wood bead, just as artisans in very ancient cultures did centuries ago. Go outside, find a nice fat stick, and whittle a bead. Hopefully you will have an occasion to do so while sitting on your porch swing as you watch the sun set.

Decorated Ceramic Beads

Ceramic clay and porcelain are often molded or formed into beads. Some are then decorated with glazes and then fired; others are painted with permanent colors after firing with a simple glaze. Decals are frequently added to the surface of the fired ceramic bead. In Peru, artisans add beautiful painted geometric designs to fired clay beads.

Shapes and sizes are nearly unlimited, and colors are literally unrestricted. One thing to consider when using ceramic beads is that they can be quite heavy. Try combining them with lighter-weight materials for better wearability.

Faceted Glass Beads

Often loosely called "crystals," faceted glass beads are made in many different shapes and colors. Two principal methods are used to make faceted glass beads. Molded beads of this type are called "firepolish" because they are treated with heat after molding to create the beautiful smooth finish and clean edges of the beads. They are made from plain glass and are generally available in a wider range of colors and finishes than Austrian- and Czech-cut crystal. Although cut crystal is expensive because it is a time-consuming process compared to molding and uses a better grade of glass, there is a wider range of shapes available.

Finishes can be applied to any faceted glass. The most common is known as Aurora Borealis (AB) finish, which is an iridescent, predominantly green, film applied to the surface of the bead after it is cut or molded. Firepolish beads are available with metallic finishes, often sprayed onto half of the surface of the bead, usually in silver or bronze.

Common shapes of faceted beads.

   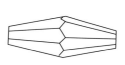

Semi-Precious Stones

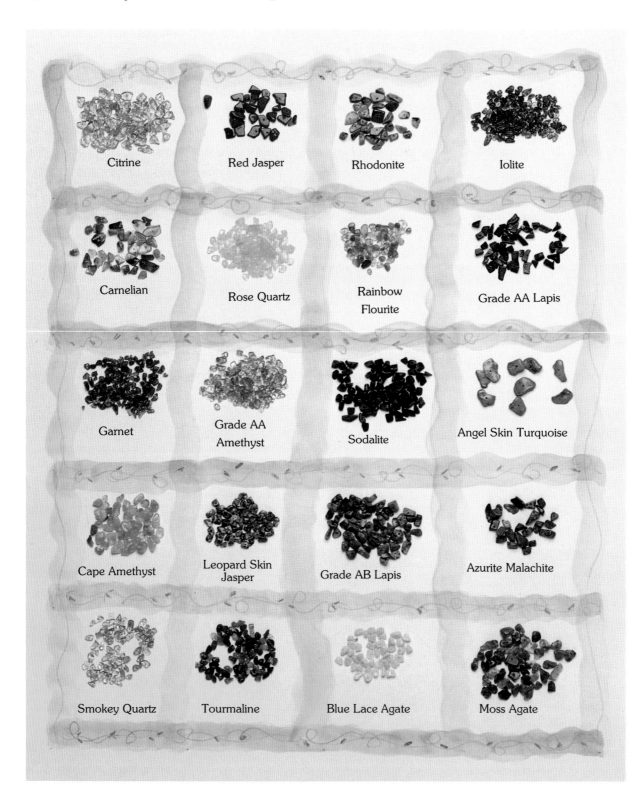

Citrine

Red Jasper

Rhodonite

Iolite

Carnelian

Rose Quartz

Rainbow Flourite

Grade AA Lapis

Garnet

Grade AA Amethyst

Sodalite

Angel Skin Turquoise

Cape Amethyst

Leopard Skin Jasper

Grade AB Lapis

Azurite Malachite

Smokey Quartz

Tourmaline

Blue Lace Agate

Moss Agate

20

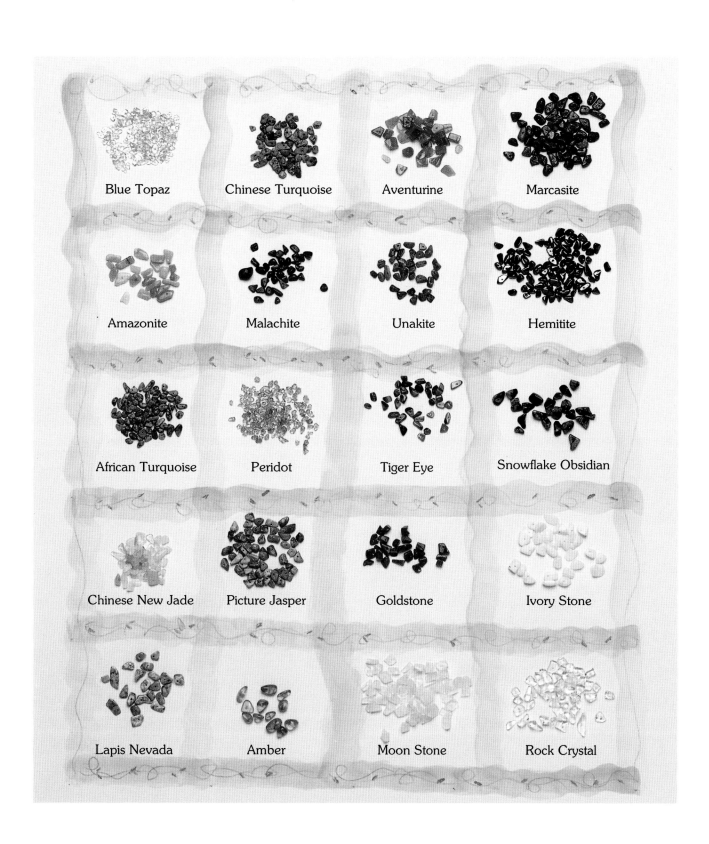

Blue Topaz

Chinese Turquoise

Aventurine

Marcasite

Amazonite

Malachite

Unakite

Hemitite

African Turquoise

Peridot

Tiger Eye

Snowflake Obsidian

Chinese New Jade

Picture Jasper

Goldstone

Ivory Stone

Lapis Nevada

Amber

Moon Stone

Rock Crystal

Beading Components

Ear Findings

Ear findings are available in a wide range of styles and sizes. They can be made of plated base metal or genuine gold and silver. Brightly colored niobium is regularly used to enhance the look of a pair of earrings; it is especially effective when used in combination with niobium wire.

Knot Ends

Knot ends are used to join a strand of beads to some other component. The small top loop is closed over the knot in the fiber; you may need to double or even triple the knot to make sure it stays within the end. Frequently a knot end is attached to a ring which is then attached to a clasp.

Headpins and Eyepins

Headpins are the most commonly used component in earrings. They come in a variety of gauges, finishes and lengths. The very narrow .21 gauge is ideal for freshwater pearls, while the .28 gauge is for beads with larger holes. Headpins look much like nails, with one flat end which keeps the beads from falling off. To use them, simply thread on your beads and cut the headpin with wirecutters so there is ¼" to ⅜" left unbeaded. Use round-nose pliers to make a loop in the top of the pin, then close it around the intended finding. Eyepins are used in the same manner as headpins, but have a loop instead of a flat end. A headpin with beads can be attached to the eyepin, and will dangle with a nice movement. Many eyepins can be beaded and joined together to form a necklace or bracelet.

Clasps

Clasps can be very ornate or quite simple; because they are usually relatively large, they can act as part of the design itself. So the size, finish and design of the clasp should be coordinated with your beadwork if possible.

Crimps

Crimps are flattened over wire or leather to secure a strand of beads to a clasp or other finding. Coordinate the finish of the crimp with the finish of the clasp for a nice look; be sure the crimp is the proper size for the material being secured.

Rings

Rings are used to join other components, such as clasps or strung beads. They are available in a wide range of sizes and finishes. Jump rings have a gap in the circle and separate easily with pliers. Split rings are tiny key holders; the ring is doubled onto itself for better surety. They are a bit more difficult to use than jump rings.

Bead Sizes

#3 Bugles

#10mm Round

30mm Bugles

6/0 Seed Beads

11/0 Seed Beads

Antique Beads

#1 Bugles

20mm Bugles

15mm Bugles

#5 Bugles

25mm Bugles

4mm Round

8/0 Seed Beads

6mm Round

14/0 Seed Beads

Hex Beads

12mm Round

10/0 Seed Beads

5mm Round

#2 Bugles

Bead Finishes

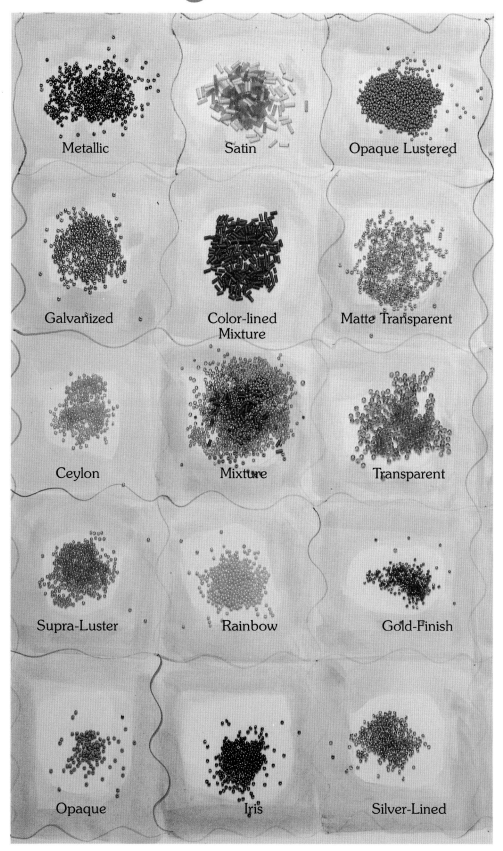

Metallic

Satin

Opaque Lustered

Galvanized

Color-lined Mixture

Matte Transparent

Ceylon

Mixture

Transparent

Supra-Luster

Rainbow

Gold-Finish

Opaque

Iris

Silver-Lined

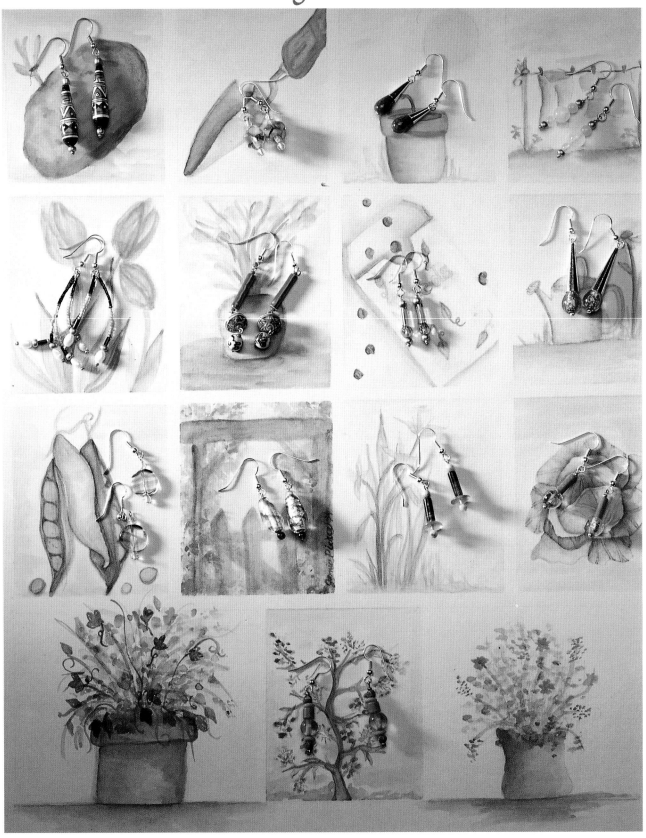

Materials needed to make earrings shown on pages 26 and 27.

---

2 gold-tone earwires
4 metallic gold 6/0 seed beads
2 gold-tone headpins
2 metallic gold 11/0 seed beads

---

2 sterling silver earwires
2 sterling silver headpins
2 bi-cone artglass beads, approximately 12mm long
4 pale pink 4mm round glass
  beads

---

2 sterling silver earwires
2 sterling silver headpins
2 12mm sterling silver cone ends
2 ceramic teardrop-shaped beads,
  approximately 15mm

---

2 gold-tone earwires
4 metallic gold 6/0 seed beads
2 metallic gold 11/0 seed beads
2 gold-tone headpins
4 rose quartz beads, 6mm round
2 rose quartz beads, 10mm round

---

2 gold-tone earwires
6 gold-tone headpins (narrow
  gauge, .21 if possible)
6 metallic gold 6/0 seed beads
12 metallic gold 11/0 seed beads
6 11/0 seed beads each:
  pale yellow, lt. orange, med.
  orange, peach, rose, lavender,
  light blue, aqua
About 80 black hex beads
6 freshwater pearls, about
  4-4.5 mm

---

2 silver earwires
4 silver-tone eyepins
2 silver-tone headpins
2 cobalt ceramic tubes, about
  4mm x 20mm
12 cobalt 11/0 seed beads
2 cobalt and white ceramic
  beads, 8mm round
2 cobalt and white ceramic
  beads, flat bicone,
  12mm x 8mm

---

2 gold-tone earwires
4 metallic gold 6/0 seed beads
4 metallic gold 11/0 seed beads
2 lt. blue AB 6mm fire-polish
  crystals
2 lt. blue AB tubes, about
  3mm x 10mm
2 gold-tone headpins

---

2 sterling silver earwires
2 sterling silver cone ends, about
  25mm long
2 teardrop-shaped lamp beads,
  about 10mm x 14mm
2 sterling silver headpins
2 metallic silver 11/0 seed beads

---

2 silver earwires
2 silver-tone headpins
2 flat discs with vertical hole, artglass, about 12mm
4 pale pink glass beads, 4mm
  round

---

2 silver-tone earwires
2 silver-tone headpins
2 garnet beads, 4mm round
2 hand-blown glass beads, silver
  and maroon, 25mm teardrop

---

2 silver-tone earwires
2 silver-tone headpins
2 flourite tubes, about 14mm long
2 flourite flat discs, about 10mm
  diameter
4 tree agate beads, 4mm round

---

2 sterling silver earwires
2 hand-blown glass beads, rose
  and silver, 10mm round
4 metallic silver 11/0 seed beads
2 ceramic tubes, about 12mm
  long, matte rose
2 sterling silver headpins

2 gold-tone earwires
2 gold-tone headpins
4 metallic bronze 11/0 seed beads
2 amber glass beads, 10mm round
4 olive glass English-cut, 4mm
4 beige ceramic flat donuts, 6mm
2 med. brown ceramic tubes,
  6mm

2 gold-plated earwires
2 gold-plated headpins
6 metallic gold 6/0 seed beads
4 metallic gold 11/0 seed beads
2 rose quartz tubes, about 14mm long
2 diamond-shaped cloisonne beads, vertical hole

2 gold-tone earwires
2 gold-tone headpins
4 metallic gold 11/0 seed beads
4 rose glass beads, 4mm round
2 synthetic clay beads, floral design, about 24mm diameter, vertical hole

2 silver-tone earwires
6 silver-tone headpins
6 turquoise chips
6 silver metallic 6/0 seed beads
18 metallic silver 11/0 seed beads
12 opaque aqua 11/0 seed beads
84 opaque black 11/0 seed beads

2 gold-tone earwires
2 gold-tone headpins
4 metallic gold 11/0 seed beads
4 lt. topaz AB fire-polish beads, 4mm
2 cloisonne tubes, about 20mm long

2 gold-tone earwires
4 metallic gold 6/0 seed beads
4 metallic gold 11/0 seed beads
2 gold-tone headpins
2 knotted synthetic clay beads, about 18mm diameter

2 silver-tone earwires
2 silver-tone headpins
6 lustered rose 6/0 seed beads
2 metallic silver 11/0 seed beads
2 flourite tubes, about 14mm long
2 pale green glass beads, 10mm round

2 gold-tone earwires
2 gold-tone headpins
4 metallic gold 6/0 seed beads
2 metallic gold 11/0 seed beads
2 ceramic tubes, about 12mm x 6mm
2 ceramic flat disks, vertical hole about 18mm

2 gold-tone earwires
2 gold-tone headpins (narrow gauge, .21 if available)
4 silver-lined gold 11/0 seed beads
2 turquoise tubes, about 15mm long
2 freshwater pearls, about 4mm
2 leopard skin jasper beads, 8mm round

2 sterling silver earwires
2 sterling silver headpins
4 matte lt. blue 6/0 seed beads
4 flat disks, matte rose streaked with blue, 6mm
4 flat donuts, matte lavender, 8mm
2 flat cylinders, 6mm x 8mm, matte rose streaked with red

2 gold-tone earwires
2 gold-tone headpins
4 goldstone beads, 4mm round
2 handblown beads, purple glass streaked with goldstone, 10mm round

2 gold-tone earwires
2 gold-tone headpins
2 rectangular white bone beads, about 6mm x 6mm x 12mm
2 flat carved dark brown bone beads, about 10mm diameter
2 round donut med. brown bone beads, about 8mm
4 gold-tone metallic beads, about 3mm

2 silver-tone earwires
2 silver-tone headpins
16 metallic silver 11/0 seed beads
4 opaque aqua 8/0 seed beads
4 opaque black 6/0 seed beads
2 flourite beads, 10mm round

2 silver-tone earwires
2 silver-tone headpins
2 rose quartz tubes, about 14mm long
2 lapis nevada beads, about 8mm round
2 tree agate beads, about 4mm round

2 gold-tone earwires
2 gold-tone headpins
4 tigereye beads, 4mm round
2 long carved lt. brown bone beads, about 30mm long

❀ *Mille Fleur* ❀ *Mille Fleur* ❀ *Mille Fleur* ❀ *Mille Fleur* ❀ *Mille Fleur* ❀

Mille Fleur
B R A C E L E T

Materials

3 oz. of silver-lined crystal 12/0 3-cut beads

100 metallic gold 12/0 3-cut beads

13 floral lamp or glass beads, assorted sizes and colors

¼" satin cord; length of wrist plus 1"

One gold-tone spring clasp

One ¼" gold-tone jump ring

Matching thread

Directions

1. Weave beadwork according to Mille Fleur Pattern; see "Squared Needleweaving" on page 115. Repeat until desired length is reached.

2. Form a tube around satin cord and cap end using silver-lined crystals; see "Finishing a Tube" on page 122.

3. Stitch spring clasp and jump ring to opposite ends of finished tube.

4. Attach lamp beads, spacing evenly around bracelet; see Diagram 1.

Mille Fleur Pattern

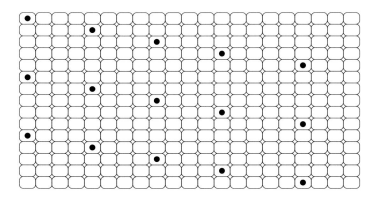

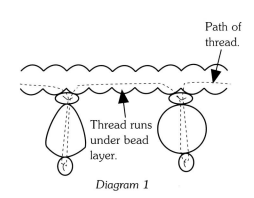

Path of thread.

Thread runs under bead layer.

Diagram 1

────── KEY ──────

○ metallic gold

◉ silver-lined crystal

Black & White
PIN AND EARRING SET

Materials

11/0 seed beads:
    92 black opaque
    108 lustered white
    330 silver metallic
    150 matte smokey rainbow
20 metallic silver 6/0 seed beads
Six 4-4.5mm freshwater pearls
Three white 6mm AB faceted
    firepolish crystals

3" x 3" fabric piece for backing
1½" pinback
Earclips or post mountings
Two doubled-faced adhesive dots for
    earrings
Matching thread

Directions

1. Beginning at foundation row, weave design pieces according to Black and White Pin and Earrings Patterns; see "Brick Stitch" on page 119.

2. Turn diamonds so beads have long side vertical. Add hangers where indicated. Bury excess threads within·weave; clip close.

3. Attach backing fabric to pin; see "Attaching Backing" on page 123. Attach pinback.

4. Apply double-faced adhesive pads to earring mountings. Center beadwork over mountings and press to secure.

Foundation row

Pin

Foundation row

Earrings
Make two.

=== KEY ===

● 11/0 black opaque
□ 11/0 lustered white
□ 11/0 silver metallic
▨ 11/0 matte smokey rainbow
⬭ 6/0 metallic silver

⬭ freshwater pearls

◯ white firepolish crystals

Black & White
Pin and Earrings
Patterns

Beaded Bouquet
CLUTCH BAG

Materials

11/0 seed beads:
- 112 lt. orchid
- 374 transparent dark green
- 127 transparent med. green
- 125 lustered lt. green
- 275 lustered lt. orange
- 259 lustered lt. yellow
- 75 lustered med. purple
- 54 dark amethyst silver-lined
- 798 lustered white
- 277 lustered lt. pink
- 270 med. rose color-lined
- 346 maroon opaque

8" x 10" piece of #14 interlock needle-point canvas
Two 8" x 10" pieces of dark lightweight fabric for lining
8" x 10" piece of dark fabric for backing
Eight yards of red Persian wool
Two yards of binding trim (lightweight leather or heavy silk)
Large dark snap or magnetic closure set
Iron

Directions

1. Complete beadwork in center of canvas according to Beaded Bouquet Clutch Bag Pattern A on page 36. See "Beading on Needlepoint Canvas" on page 110.

2. Trace Beaded Bouquet Clutch Bag Pattern B found on page 37 onto tracing paper. Center it over bead-work and mark outline with pencil. Stitch background within this oval using Persian wool in basketweave stitch; see "Stitching Needlepoint" on page 111.

3. Stretch beadwork back to original shape using the steam from the iron. Trim excess canvas to ¼".

4. Using trimmed piece as a template, cut two pieces of lining and one piece of backing.

5. Baste wrong side of beadwork to one lining piece. Slipstitch bias trim around edges; see Diagram 1.

6. Baste remaining lining piece and backing piece together. Slipstitch bias trim around edges.

7. With wrong sides together, join front piece to back, leaving a 7" opening at top; see Diagram 2.

8. Turn inside out. Attach closure set.

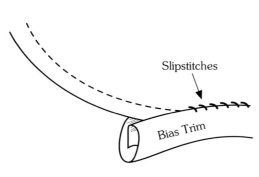

Diagram 1

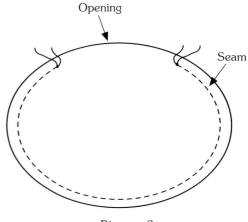

Diagram 2

Beaded Bouquet Clutch Bag Pattern A

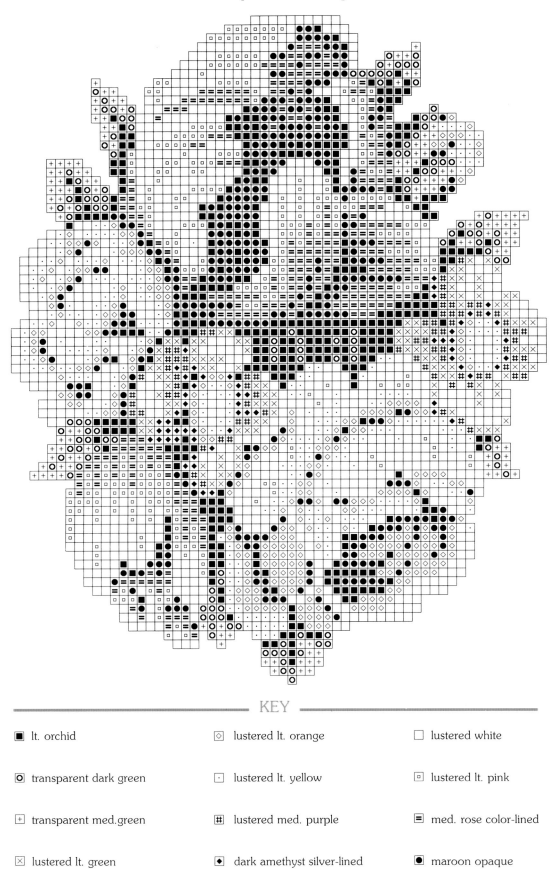

■	lt. orchid	⊙	lustered lt. orange	☐	lustered white
◙	transparent dark green	·	lustered lt. yellow	⊡	lustered lt. pink
⊞	transparent med. green	♯	lustered med. purple	=	med. rose color-lined
☒	lustered lt. green	◆	dark amethyst silver-lined	●	maroon opaque

36

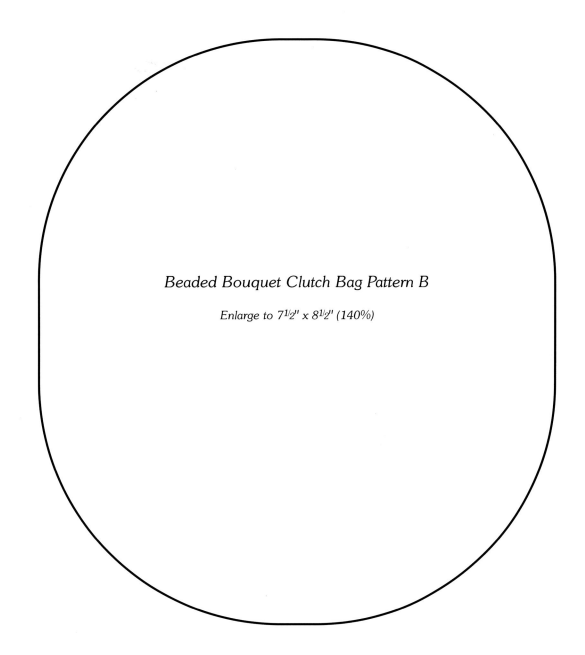

Beaded Bouquet Clutch Bag Pattern B

Enlarge to $7^{1/2}''$ x $8^{1/2}''$ (140%)

The designer grants permission to photo-copy patterns found in this book.

❀ *Cobalt & Gold* ❀ *Cobalt & Gold* ❀ *Cobalt & Gold* ❀ *Cobalt & Gold* ❀ *Cobalt & Gold* ❀

Cobalt & Gold
CABOCHON EARRINGS

Materials

Two 25mm x 18mm frosted or high-gloss acrylic cabochons
450 silver-lined gold 11/0 seed beads
Two 5mm x 7mm cobalt blue teardrop crystals

Two 6mm cobalt blue faceted crystals
Six silver-lined gold 6/0 seed beads
Earring mountings
Gold thread (non-metallic)

Directions

1. Encase both cabochons in silver-lined gold beads; see "Cabochon Collectibles" on page 74.

2. Bring out thread at bottom center of frame and make the hangers; see Diagram 1.

3. Bury the thread in the frame of the cabochon until secure; clip close to knot.

4. Attach to earring mountings.

KEY

⬭ 11/0 silver-lined gold

⬯ 6/0 silver-lined gold

⬡ 6mm cobalt crystal

⬠ 5mm x 7mm cobalt teardrops

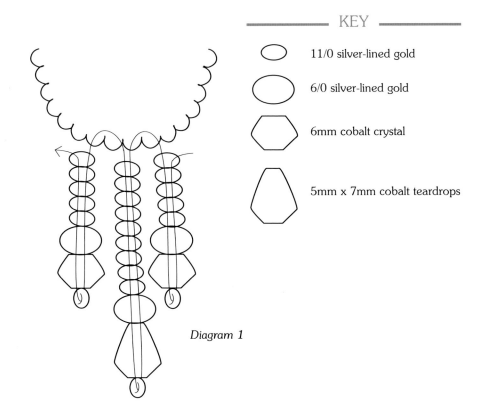

Diagram 1

Delft
KNOTTED NECKLACE

Materials

Enough assorted graduated blue and white decorated ceramic beads to make a 22" necklace

Two yards of matching blue medium-weight rayon fiber

One silver clasp
Two silver jump rings
Matching blue thread
Glue

Directions

1. Arrange beads in pleasing order.

2. String first bead. Make a knot after bead. Make another knot directly over first so it appears to be a very large single knot. Repeat until all beads are strung.

3. Rework last knot four times so that it is larger than other knots. Apply a coating of glue to knot; let dry. Trim fiber very close to knot. Attach jump rings to both sides. Attach clasp to jump rings; see "Finishing Techniques" on page 102.

4. Trim excess rayon and thread.

To create the lovely effect in this necklace, one large bead was placed at the center. The beads were then strung on both sides in an identical pattern.

❂ *Isis* ❂ *Isis* ❂ *Isis* ❂ *Isis* ❂ *Isis* ❂ *Isis* ❂ *Isis* ❂ *Isis* ❂ *Isis* ❂

Isis
PIN

Materials

12/0 3-cut beads:
   60 dark beige
   450 black
   100 lt. beige (or topaz)
   20 dark rose
   12 white
   One hank metallic gold
   One hank cream
10/0 seed beads:
   72 med. blue opaque
   90 coral opaque

60 matte aqua iris #2 bugle beads
Six turquoise chips
Two lapis chips
Two tubes turquoise 4mm x 10mm
80 med. blue hex beads
100 aqua hex beads
One 5" x 5" fabric piece for backing
One 3" x 4" fusible webbing piece
One 1½" pinback
One 5" x 5" bead card
Matching thread

Directions

1. Transfer Isis Pin Pattern on page 44 to bead card.

2. Sew beads to card according to Isis Pin Pattern in the following order:
   a. lapis and turquoise chips.
   b. lines of metallic gold 12/0 3-cut.
   c. matte aqua iris #2 bugle beads.
   d. 10/0 med. blue opaque, 10/0 coral opaque, blue hexes and aqua hexes.
   e. black 12/0 3-cut for eyes. Fill spaces inside eyes with white 12/0 3-cut.
   f. sew on lips, then sew on dark and lt. beige 12/0 3-cut in face.
   g. fill open spaces in face with cream 12/0 3-cut.
   h. black 12/0 3-cut.

3. Make strands; see Diagram 1. Bring needle up through card at letter. Thread on beads, then run needle back through beads. Bring needle back through wrong side of card, then up again through next letter.

4. Fuse backing fabric to stitched bead card; see "Fusing" on page 106.

5. Trim excess card/fabric. Attach pinback.

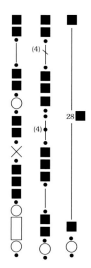

Diagram 1
Hanging Strands
(see next page for key)

Isis Pin Pattern

=== KEY ===

Ⓣ turquoise chips	⟋⟍ lines of aqua hexes
Ⓛ lapis chips	⟋⟍⟍ lines of dark beige 12/0 3-cut
— lines of metallic gold 12/0 3-cut	⟋⊖⟍ lines of lt. beige 12/0 3-cut
• individual metallic gold 12/0 3-cut	▲ individual dark beige 12/0 3-cut
▬ matte aqua iris #2 bugle beads	△ individual lt. beige 12/0 3-cut
✕ individual med. blue opaque 10/0	▢ individual dark rose 12/0 3-cut
○ individual coral opaque 10/0	▬▬ lines of black 12/0 3-cut
⟋•⟍ lines of med. blue hexes	▮ individual black 12/0 3-cut

❀ *Fruit Loops* ❀ *Fruit Loops* ❀ *Fruit Loops* ❀ *Fruit Loops* ❀ *Fruit Loops* ❀

Fruit Loops
NECKLACE

Materials

Six assorted 12mm fruit-shaped beads
  with loops
11/0 seed beads:
  90 lustered pale yellow
  100 lustered pale orange
  120 lustered lt. green
6/0 seed beads:
  88 coral matte
  40 yellow matte
6mm round glass beads:
  34 yellow matte
  20 lt. green matte

6mm flat donut beads:
  32 lt. salmon
  40 aqua ceramic
32 (4mm) opaque green English-cut
  beads
16 (6mm x 6mm) aqua ceramic tubes
Two one-inch headpins
One gold-finish spring clasp with ring
Two gold-finish end caps
Lightweight nylon
Glue

Directions

1. Cut three 24" lengths of nylon.

2. String beads onto the nylon thread according to Fruit Loops Necklace Pattern.

3. Gather excess strands from one side of necklace and tie in a simple knot. Repeat over first knot. Repeat for other side, ensuring all slack is taken up from strands.

4. Place dab of glue on knots at both ends. Trim excess nylon to ¼". Let dry.

5. Trim flat head off both headpins. Twist one end of each into a small open loop. Close loop around knots at both ends of necklace.

6. Insert unlooped end of headpin through hole in beadcap so knot and loop disappear into cap; see Diagram 1. Cut protruding end of headpin ⅜" above the cap. Twist into open loop. Close one loop around clasp and other around ring.

Diagram 1
Detail of End Cap

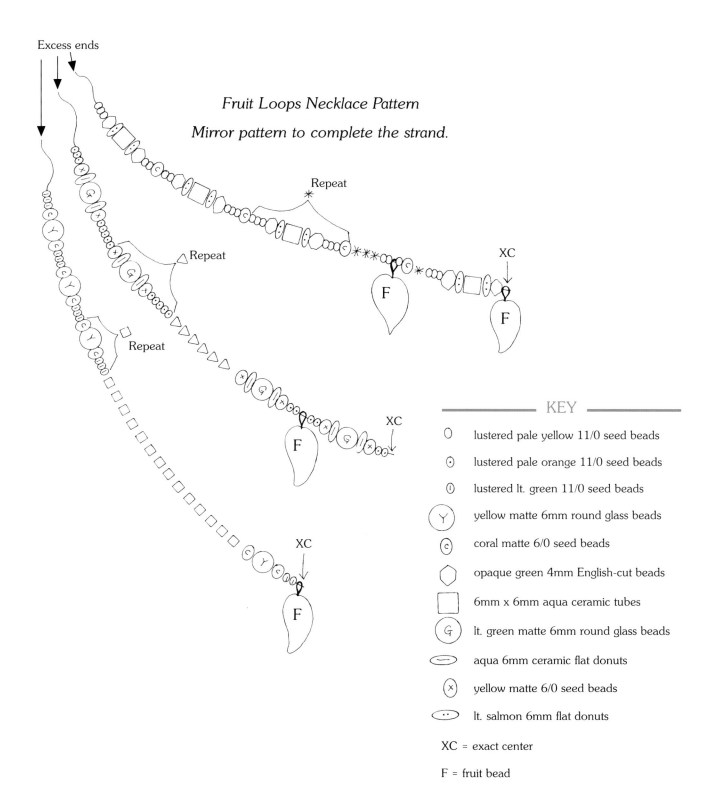

Excess ends

Fruit Loops Necklace Pattern

Mirror pattern to complete the strand.

Repeat

Repeat

Repeat

XC

XC

XC

F

F

F

F

F

======= KEY =======

○ lustered pale yellow 11/0 seed beads

⊙ lustered pale orange 11/0 seed beads

⓪ lustered lt. green 11/0 seed beads

Ⓨ yellow matte 6mm round glass beads

ⓒ coral matte 6/0 seed beads

⬡ opaque green 4mm English-cut beads

☐ 6mm x 6mm aqua ceramic tubes

Ⓖ lt. green matte 6mm round glass beads

⬭ aqua 6mm ceramic flat donuts

⊗ yellow matte 6/0 seed beads

⬮ lt. salmon 6mm flat donuts

XC = exact center

F = fruit bead

Five~Strands ❀ *Five~Strands* ❀ *Five~Strands* ❀ *Five~Strands* ❀ *Five~Strands* ❀

Five-Strands
TWISTED NECKLACE

Materials

11/0 seed beads (amounts are approximates):
  - 600 silver-lined aqua
  - 500 silver-lined pink
  - 550 silver-lined gold
  - 350 silver-lined lt. amethyst
95 lustered pink 6/0 seed beads
80 metallic gold 6/0 seed beads
31 lt. sapphire AB 6mm fire-polish crystals
62 lt. amethyst AB 4mm glass balls
42 (3-4mm) freshwater pearls

130 silver-lined aqua #2 bugle beads
40 transparent pink 6mm glass balls
40 transparent aqua 6mm glass balls
45 lt. blue opaque 4mm beads English-cut
90 lt. amethyst 4mm English-cut beads
One necklace-shortening clasp
Eight yards of lightweight nylon thread
Glue

Directions

1. String five separate 38"-long strands of beads according to Five-Strands Pattern. See "Endless Loops" on page 126.

2. Tie each strand with a square knot. Dab knot with glue. Let dry. Bury thread ends in beadwork. Clip excess.

Five-Strands Pattern

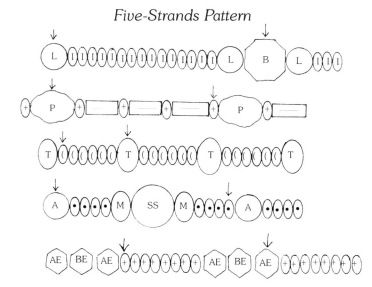

Design pattern repeats between arrows.

─────── KEY ───────

T   lustered pink 6/0 seed beads
(silver-lined aqua 11/0 seed beads
B   lt. sapphire AB 6mm fire-polish crystals
L   lt. amethyst AB 4mm glass balls
I   silver-lined pink 11/0 seed beads
P   3-4mm freshwater pearls
+   silver-lined gold 11/0 seed beads
—   silver-lined aqua #2 bugle beads
SS   transparent pink 6mm glass balls
A   transparent aqua 6mm glass balls
M   metallic gold 6/0 seed beads
•   silver-lined lt. amethyst 11/0 seed beads
BE   lt. blue opaque 4mm English-cut beads
AE   lt. amethyst 4mm English-cut beads

"Eye" Lights
EYEPIN NECKLACE AND EARRINGS

Materials

148 metallic gold 11/0 seed beads
76 metallic gold 6/0 seed beads
48 iris #2 bugle beads
16 (6mm) green iris fire-polish
Sixteen 2" gold-finish eyepins

Two 1" gold-finish eyepins
Two gold-finish ear findings with bottom loop
One gold-finish clasp
Round-nose pliers

Directions

Necklace:

1. Thread twelve 2" eyepins for necklace; see Diagram 1. Trim unlooped end to 3/16" beyond last bead.

2. Using round-nose pliers, join necklace eyepins by closing unlooped end of one pin around looped end of another until all twelve are joined. Join clasp to eyepin chain at last loops of chain.

Earrings:

1. Thread beads onto remaining eyepins and headpins; see Diagrams 2, 3, and 4.

2. Curve two 1" eyepins. Trim unbeaded ends to 3/8".

3. Join components together with loops and attach to ear findings; see Diagram 5.

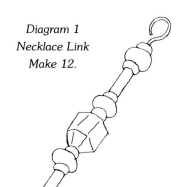

Diagram 1
Necklace Link
Make 12.

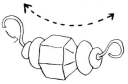
Curve slightly.

Diagram 2
Earring Bottom Space
Make two.

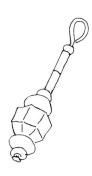

Diagram 3
Earring Center Drop
Make two on headpin.

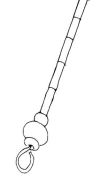

Diagram 4
Earring Side Leg
Make four.

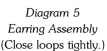

Diagram 5
Earring Assembly
(Close loops tightly.)

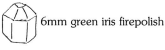
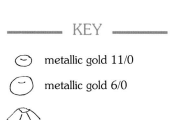

⊛ *Brick Stitch* ⊛ *Brick Stitch* ⊛ *Brick Stitch* ⊛ *Brick Stitch* ⊛ *Brick Stitch* ⊛

Brick Stitch
BARRETTE

Materials

11/0 seed beads:
  168 silver metallic
  98 black opaque
  68 lustered pale aqua
  61 lustered med. aqua

2" x 4" piece fabric for backing
2" barrette blank
Index card
Matching thread

Directions

1. Weave design piece according to Brick Stitch Barrette Pattern; see "Brick Stitch" on page 119.

2. Attach backing fabric and index card to beadwork; see "Attaching Backing" on page 123.

3. Attach beadwork to barrette blank.

Foundation row

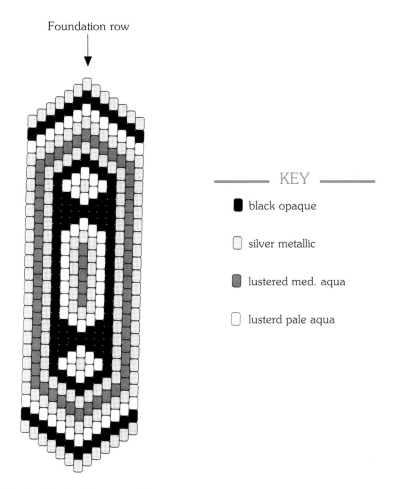

KEY

▇ black opaque

▢ silver metallic

▨ lustered med. aqua

▢ lusterd pale aqua

Brick Stitch Barrette Pattern

⊛ *Fancy Stix* ⊛ *Fancy Stix* ⊛ *Fancy Stix* ⊛ *Fancy Stix* ⊛ *Fancy Stix* ⊛

Fancy Stix
STICK PINS

Assorted beads to make a length of 1½" to 2½"
One 4" to 5" stick pin
One crimp bead

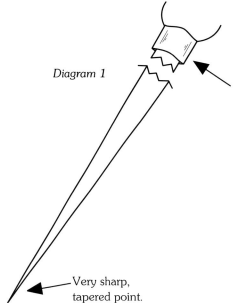

Diagram 1

Crimp should fit snugly and flatten only slightly. If the crimp is too large it flattens unattractively and may slip.

Very sharp, tapered point.

Directions

1. Slide beads onto end of stick pin. Hold in place with crimp bead; see Diagram 1.

What's wonderful about these stick pins is that you can coordinate the beads to match any outfit you own—the possibilities are endless!

When choosing a stick pin, remember that it must be very sharp at the pointed end to insure it will not damage the fabric of your garment. The point should taper gradually so the fibers are spread apart rather than punctured.

Double Peyotes
B A R R E T T E

Materials

750 bronze hex beads
450 gold hex beads
1450 cream hex beads

4 dark amber 6mm rondells
9" length of ¼"-diameter cord
Barrette blank

Directions

1. Weave Double Peyotes Pattern A; see "Peyote Stitch" on page 118. Repeat with Double Peyotes Pattern B. Repeat pattern until strip is ½" longer than circumfrence of your wrist.

2. Cut cord in half. Form tube around cord with one beadwork piece; see "Finishing a Tube" on page 122. Repeat. Trim cords with beaded ends.

3. Stitch rondells to each end of finished tubes, using one gold hex bead as an anchor.

4. Stitch tubes together. Attach to barrette blank.

Double Peyotes Pattern A

— KEY —

□ bronze

☐ gold

● cream

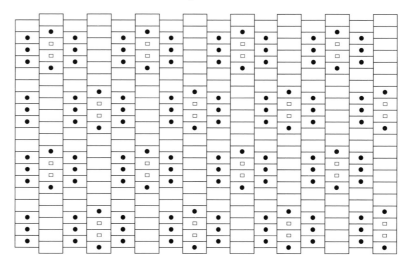

Double Peyotes Pattern B

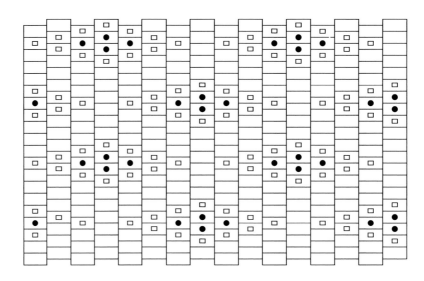

Marilyn's
PIN

Materials

14/0 seed beads:
  2 lustered opaque white
  28 lustered cream
  333 lustered pale pink
  292 lustered med. pink
  274 orchid
  198 lustered med. purple
  163 lustered med. blue
  423 blue iris
360 14/0 silver-lined crystal seed beads
  (optional for border)

4" square of 18-count interlock needle-point canvas
Two 3" square pieces of fusable webbing
3" square piece of backing fabric
12" length of satin or acetate cord
1½" pinback
Index card (unprinted)
Glue
Iron

Directions

1. Stitch beads according to Marilyn's Pin Pattern; see "Beading on Needlepoint Canvas" on page 110. If desired, also stitch silver-lined crystals around edge to form a border.

2. Stretch beadwork back to original shape using steam from iron.

3. Iron one piece of fusable webbing onto back of beadwork, centering over design. Trim excess canvas to one thread.

4. Fuse backing fabric to index card; see "Fusing" on page 106. Trim to ½" larger than trimmed beadwork.

5. Fuse beadwork to index card. Trim excess card to match beadwork.

6. Glue cord around outside edges, matching cut edges at center bottom of pin. Let dry.

7. Glue pinback to back of beadwork. Let dry.

Marilyn's Pin Pattern

○ lustered pale pink	▫ lustered med. pink
● lustered med. blue	× orchid
■ blue iris	✳ lustered med. purple
· lustered cream	▢ opaque white

⊛ *Beads on Time* ⊛ *Beads on Time* ⊛ *Beads on Time* ⊛ *Beads on Time* ⊛

Beads on Time
B E A D E D   W A T C H B A N D

Materials

Assorted beads in the colors of your
  choice (enough to make six strands
  about 2½" long); see Step 1 of
  directions.
One watch face with spring clips

Five-hole band (compatible with
  watch face)
Bracelet clasp
#0 nylon thread
Glue

Directions

1. To find size of watch band and
   amount of beads needed, measure
   wrist, minus size of watch face,
   minus 1". Divide total in half. Buy
   enough assorted beads to make six
   strands. See photo for ideas.

2. Cut six strands of nylon thread to
   size determined in Step 1, adding 3".

3. Make beaded strands; see Diagram
   1. Thread ends through five-hole
   band; tie and glue. Let dry.

4. Thread other ends through clasp.
   Thread ends back through beads; tie
   and glue. Let dry.

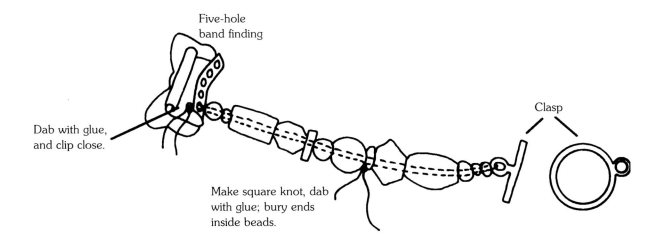

Five-hole
band finding

Dab with glue,
and clip close.

Make square knot, dab
with glue; bury ends
inside beads.

Clasp

Diagram 1

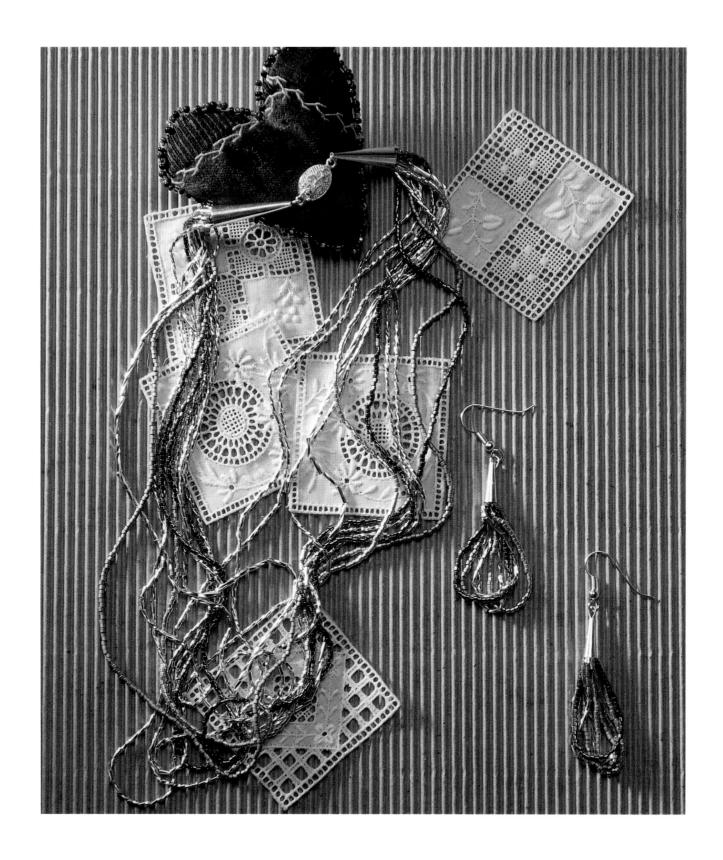

Silver Loops
NECKLACE AND EARRINGS

Materials

Purchase amounts adequate to string strands in lengths indicated:

¼" sterling silver tubes (two 22" strands and two 3" strands)

⅛" sterling silver tubes (two 22" strands and two 3" strands)

Galvanized gold Delicas or hex beads (two 22" strands)

Matte stainless steel Delicas or hex beads (one 22" strand)

Bronze metallic Delicas or hex beads (one 22" strand)

Purple iris Delicas or hex beads (one 22" strand)

Delica beads:
    purple iris (one 3" strand)
    gold (one 3" strand)
    galvanized gold (one 3" strand)

Two ⅛" silver stainless steel Delicas

Two 13mm sterling silver cone ends

Two sterling silver earwires

Two sterling silver 1" headpins

Two 25mm sterling silver cone ends

Sterling silver clasp

10 yards of #2 nylon thread

Directions

Necklace:

1. Cut nine lengths of nylon each 30" long.

2. String beads so each strand equals 22".

3. Tie all nine lengths together into a knot at both ends, making sure to take up all slack in each strand before tying.

4. Soak knot in glue, then trim excess to ½". Let dry.

5. Trim flat end off headpin using wire-cutters. Twist one end into a loop, then close the loop around one knot; see Diagram 1.

6. Insert the untwisted end through the 25mm cone, then trim headpin to ⅜". Form a loop with this end and close loop around one side of clasp. Repeat on other side with other side of clasp.

Earrings:

1. Cut ten strands of nylon each 6" long and string on beads so the total length of beads is 3". Make one strand of each color bead for each earring.

2. For each earring, gather together all ends of all five strands and tie into one knot to form a curved loop.

3. Soak knot in glue and trim excess nylon to ⅜". Let dry.

4. Form loop and insert through end cone as for necklace, but attach outer loop to base of each earwire.

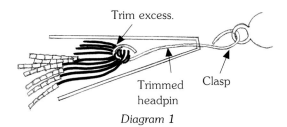

Trim excess.

Trimmed headpin

Clasp

Diagram 1

❀ *Five Cats* ❀ *Five Cats* ❀ *Five Cats* ❀ *Five Cats* ❀ *Five Cats* ❀

Five Cats
NECKLACE AND EARRINGS

Materials

Five square purchased or handmade clay beads, with horizontal holes as follows:

Two ¾" square
Two 1" square
One 1⅛" square

Two 1" square purchased or handmade clay beads with vertical holes
Six 8mm leopard skin jasper beads
16 metallic gold 6/0 seed beads

Approximately 250 metallic gold 11/0 seed beads
One gold-finish clasp
Two gold-finish crimps
Two 1¼" gold-finish headpins
One 20" piece of tigertail
One pair gold-finish earwires

Directions

Necklace:

1. String all beads; see Diagram 1.

2. Slip one crimp over one end of tigertail and make a loop around clasp. Slide free end of tigertail into crimp, pulling until most of slack is taken up, then flatten crimp to secure tigertail. Trim excess tigertail. Repeat on opposite side. Attach clasp.

Earrings:

1. Thread beads onto both headpins and trim excess to ¼".

2. Make loop in remainder. Close loop around earwire, making sure loop is secure; see Diagram 2.

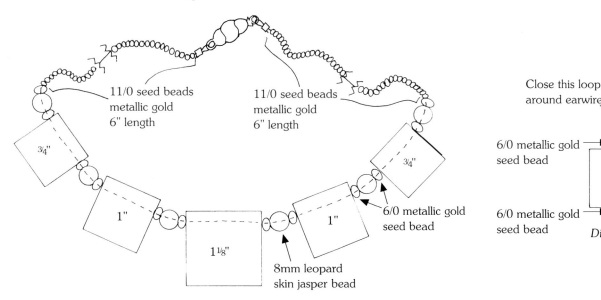

11/0 seed beads metallic gold 6" length

11/0 seed beads metallic gold 6" length

¾"

1"

1⅛"

1"

¾"

6/0 metallic gold seed bead

8mm leopard skin jasper bead

Diagram 1

Close this loop around earwire

6/0 metallic gold seed bead

6/0 metallic gold seed bead

Diagram 2

⊛ *Sunset Rose* ⊛ *Sunset Rose* ⊛ *Sunset Rose* ⊛ *Sunset Rose* ⊛ *Sunset Rose* ⊛

Sunset Rose
C L U T C H P U R S E

Materials

11/0 seed beads:
26 lustered pale yellow
26 lustered pale tangerine
39 lustered peach
58 lustered orchid
82 lustered blue-purple
78 lustered lt. blue
120 lustered dark red
250 lustered cream
350 lustered med. rose color-lined
450 lustered pale pink
350 lustered white
120 transparent dark green

220 transparent med. green rainbow
105 lustered lt. green
504 gold metallic (optional for border)
6" x 7" piece of #14 interlock needlepoint canvas
7" x 16" piece of gold metallic leather
7" x 16" piece of fabric for lining
16" length of $\frac{3}{16}$"-diameter gold metallic twisted cord
Neutral gray thread for beading
Gold thread for finishing
Iron

Directions

1. Sew beads on needlepoint according to Sunset Rose Clutch Purse Pattern; see "Beading on Needlepoint" on page 110.

2. Draw a $5\frac{1}{2}$" x $13\frac{3}{4}$" rectangle on wrong side of leather.

3. With right sides together, sew lining fabric to leather along rectangle, leaving one short side open; see Diagram 1 on page 71.

4. Trim corners. Turn bag right side out. Slipstich open end closed; see Diagram 1.

5. Fold bag in thirds. Slipstitch two sides together to form an envelope with a flap. Leave $\frac{1}{4}$" opening at bottom of each side; see Diagram 2 on page 71.

6. Slip raw end of gold trim into one opening at bottom of one side seam, then sew trim around sides and flap of bag. Bury other raw end in opening at opposite side and secure with thread; see Diagram 3 on page 71.

7. Correct any distortion in beadwork by steaming and stretching. Trim excess canvas to $\frac{3}{8}$" and clip corners. Baste all four raw edges under using invisible stitches. Press edges flat.

8. Center and stitch beadwork to flap of bag. Bury the excess thread behind beadwork; see Diagram 4 on page 71.

Sunset Rose Clutch Purse Pattern

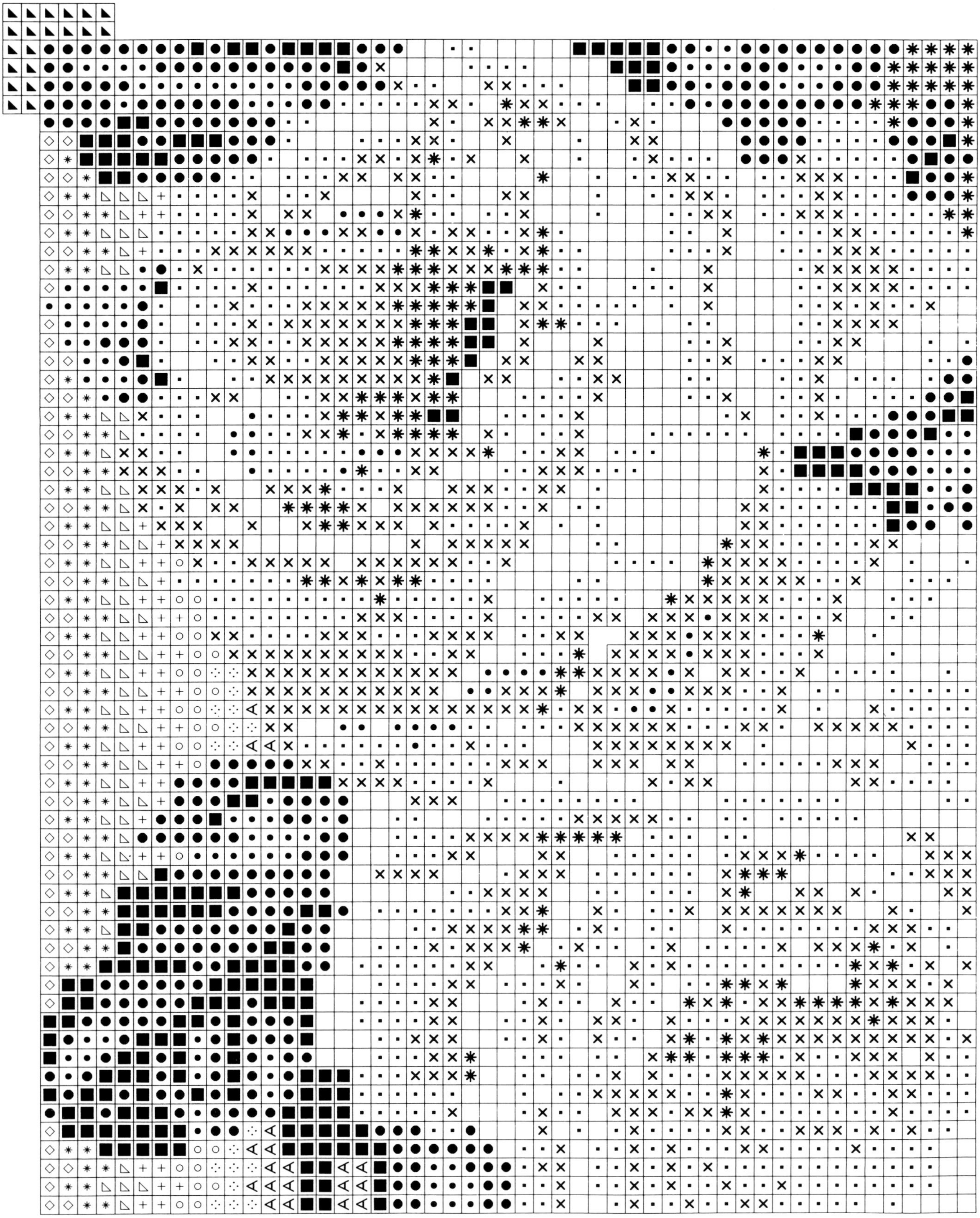

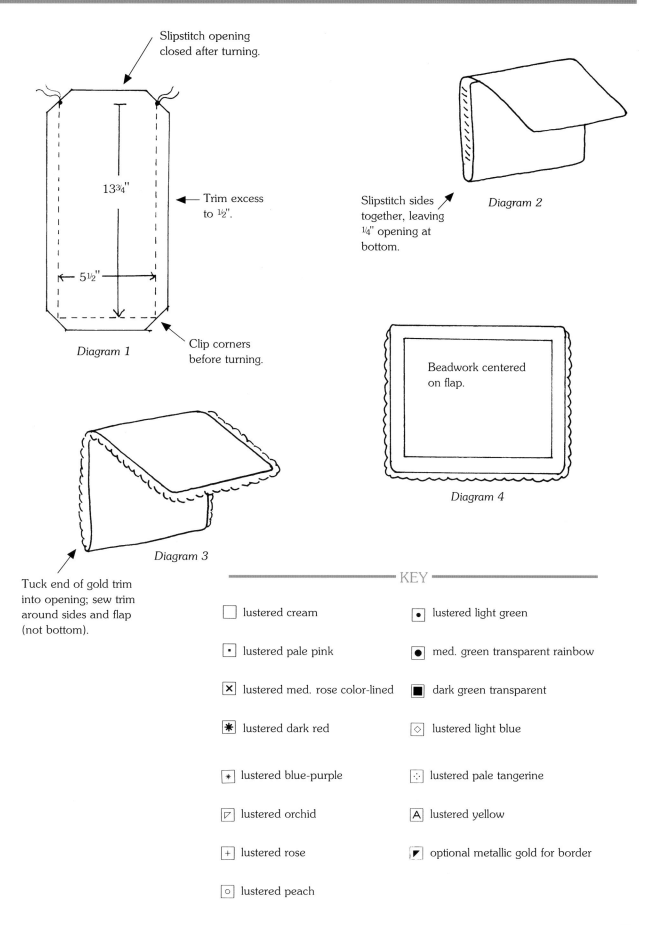

Slipstitch opening
closed after turning.

13¾"

← Trim excess
to ½".

5½"

Diagram 1

Clip corners
before turning.

Slipstitch sides
together, leaving
¼" opening at
bottom.

Diagram 2

Beadwork centered
on flap.

Diagram 4

Diagram 3

Tuck end of gold trim
into opening; sew trim
around sides and flap
(not bottom).

KEY

	lustered cream	⊡	lustered light green
⊡	lustered pale pink	⬤	med. green transparent rainbow
☒	lustered med. rose color-lined	■	dark green transparent
✳	lustered dark red	◇	lustered light blue
✳	lustered blue-purple	∴	lustered pale tangerine
▽	lustered orchid	A	lustered yellow
+	lustered rose	◢	optional metallic gold for border
○	lustered peach		

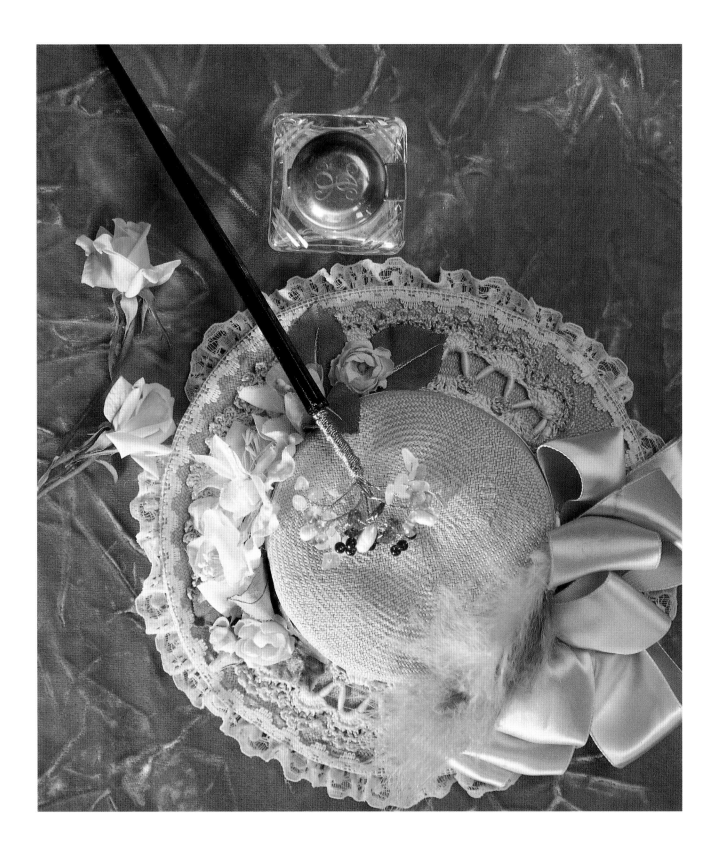

Nature's Accessories
H A I R S T I C K S

Materials

One 7"-long hairstick
Assorted beads
Instant glue

Directions

1. Remove nail from end of hairstick. Slide beads onto nail. Dip in instant glue and press firmly into hole in end of hairstick. Let dry.

All you need to make a beautiful hairstick are three or four wonderful beads and the stick itself. Most bead stores sell unbeaded hairsticks including the nail with which the beads are attached.

Cabochon Collectibles
NECKLACE AND EARRINGS

Materials

Approximately 1250 11/0 seed beads (your choice of color) for each cabochon (choose beads with consistently large holes)

One 12-14mm round bead

One packet of synthetic polymer baking clay (such as Fimo™ or Sculpey™) in the following colors:
dark aqua
dark purple
navy blue
dark maroon
dark green
lt. pink
lt. lavender
lt. sea green
lt. blue
lt. olive

One pair ear mountings
Matching thread
#0 nylon thread
Craft knife
Jewelry lacquer
Glue

Directions

Cabochons (make ten for the necklace, two each using each dark color and the light striped band; make two for the earrings using any two dark colors and the light striped band):

1. Roll out each of the five light colors to a thickness of $^1/_{16}$". Layer in any order to form a five-color band. Trim band to 1" long x $^3/_8$" high; see Diagram 1.

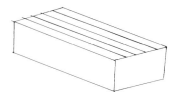

Diagram 1

2. Form two blocks of each solid dark color 1" long x $^3/_8$" high x $^1/_2$" wide.

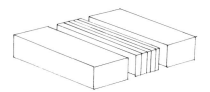

Diagram 2

3. Press solid dark bands together with light striped bands to form one rectangular block; see Diagram 2.

4. Trim block to rough octagon; see Diagram 3. Continue trimming to form domed oval; see Diagram 4.

Diagram 3

5. Smooth oval until final size is 18mm wide x 25mm long x $^1/_4$" high; see Diagram 5. Smooth with fingers.

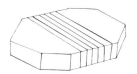

Diagram 4

6. Bake at 225° F for 20 minutes.

7. Glaze with jewelry lacquer according to manufacturer's instructions.

Diagram 5

Directions

Cabochon frame (make twelve):

1. To make one cabochon frame: Thread 45 11/0 seed beads. Wrap beaded strand around perimiter of cabochon—if strand does not completely surround perimiter, add or remove beads in multiples of three.

2. Thread second strand as first, looping every third bead; see Diagram 6. Join ends of strands to form a ring; see Diagram 7.

3. Bring thread out from any bead on either row. Work two beads in the first three beads on the band, then three beads into the next three beads; see Diagram 8. Repeat "five-looped-into-six" pattern all around.

4. Run a continuous thread through all beads in the "five-into-six" row and tighten slightly. Bring thread out in any bead on that row.

5. Loop two beads into next two beads, then two beads into next three beads; see Diagram 9. Repeat this "four-into-five" pattern all around.

6. Run a continuous thread through all beads in the "four-into-five" row, then tighten until woven beads form a "cup" with an open bottom.

7. Bring needle out in any bead on outermost 45-bead row (one of original two rows). Work two beads into first three beads, then three beads into next three beads. Continue "five-into-six" pattern all around.

8. Slip one cabochon into cup with flat side down; see Diagram 10. Run a thread through all beads in the last five-into-six row. Tighten thread until cabochon is secure. Run thread back through rows of beads until secure. Clip excess thread close.

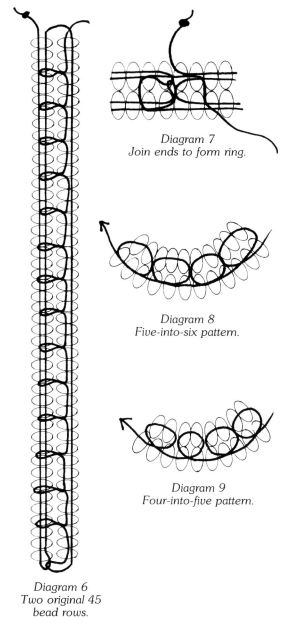

Diagram 7
Join ends to form ring.

Diagram 8
Five-into-six pattern.

Diagram 9
Four-into-five pattern.

Diagram 6
Two original 45 bead rows.

Diagram 10
Cabochon nestles in "cup."
Tighten last row with thread
to secure cabochon.

Directions

Necklace and Earrings:

1. With piece of thread three times the length of finished necklace, join cabochons together with short seed bead joiners; see Diagram 11.

2. Form loop and clasp at ends; *see* Diagram 11. Tie off with square knot. Dab with glue. Let dry. Clip and bury ends.

3. Attach one cabochon to each earring mounting.

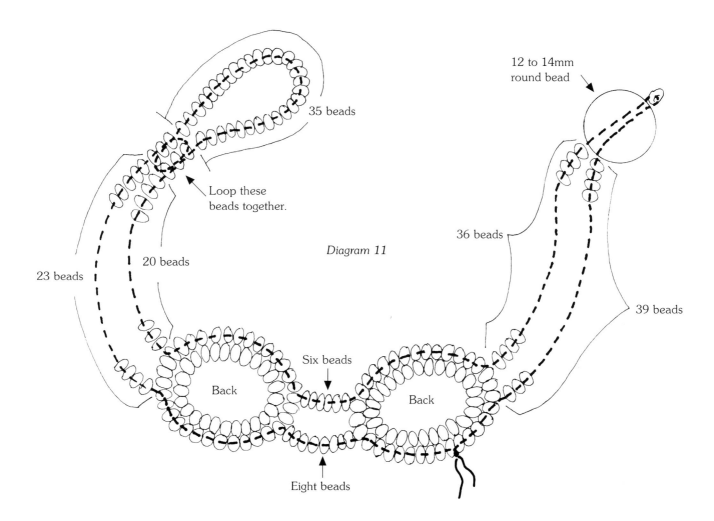

35 beads

Loop these beads together.

20 beads

23 beads

Diagram 11

Six beads

Back

Back

Eight beads

12 to 14mm round bead

36 beads

39 beads

An Heirloom ❋ An Heirloom ❋ An Heirloom ❋ An Heirloom ❋ An Heirloom ❋

An Heirloom
PIN

Materials

11/0 seed beads:
- 38 lustered cream
- 204 lustered red
- 36 lustered med. purple
- 196 silver-lined crystal
- 31 lustered pale aqua
- 308 lustered aqua
- 179 lustered pale orchid
- 63 transparent dark green rainbow

31 silver-lined crystal 15mm bugle beads
10 half-silvered 4mm English cuts
15 lustered red 6/0 seed beads
5 freshwater pearls, 4 to 4.5mm
One 4" x 2½" piece of fabric for backing
One 4" x 2½" fabric piece for lining
One 4" x 2½" piece for interfacing
One 1½" pinback

Directions

1. Weave foundation pattern according to An Heirloom Pin Pattern, using long flat edge as top of weave; see "Squared Needleweaving" on page 115.

2. Invert woven foundation pattern and add fringes from long flat edge; see pattern.

3. Attach backing; see "Backings for Odd-Shaped Pieces" on page 113.

4. Attach to pinback.

79

An Heirloom Pin Pattern

Foundation (invert after weaving)

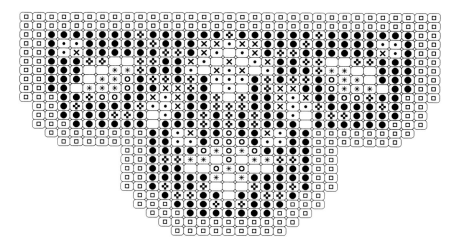

Three bottom rows of inverted foundation pattern.

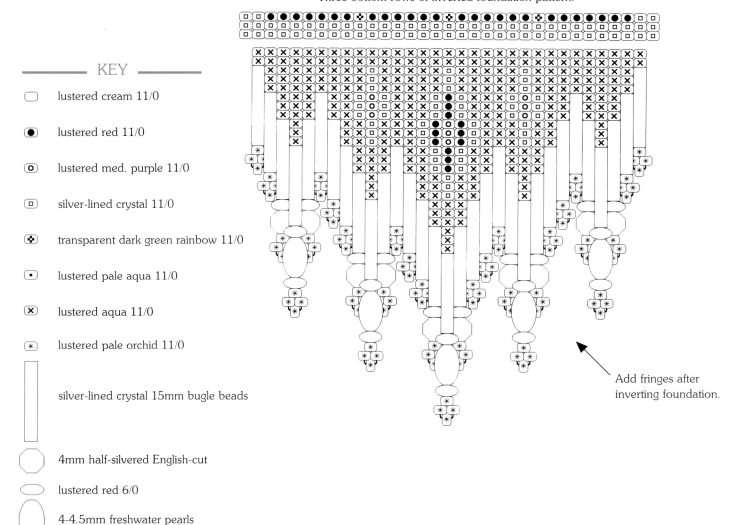

KEY

⬭ lustered cream 11/0

⊙ lustered red 11/0

⊚ lustered med. purple 11/0

⊡ silver-lined crystal 11/0

⊕ transparent dark green rainbow 11/0

⊡ lustered pale aqua 11/0

⊠ lustered aqua 11/0

✳ lustered pale orchid 11/0

▯ silver-lined crystal 15mm bugle beads

⬡ 4mm half-silvered English-cut

⬯ lustered red 6/0

⬭ 4-4.5mm freshwater pearls

Add fringes after
inverting foundation.

80

Vivé la France
FRENCH WIRE EARRINGS

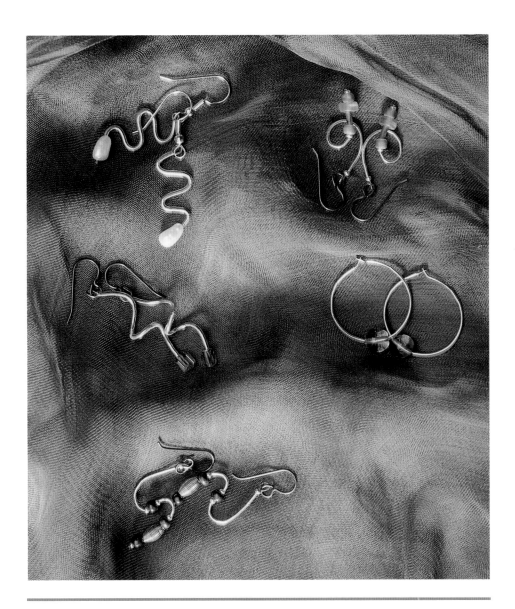

Thin filaments of gold and silver wire are neatly coiled to form French wire. This versatile material is lightweight, flexible and relatively inexpensive. It is especially useful in making earrings with headpins.

The filament used to make French wire is so fine that you can safely use scissors to cut it without fear of dulling the scissors. You must be very careful not to allow the wire to bend sharply before its final use, or it will have "kinks," much like the unruly coiled telephone wire we all know and love.

Materials

Assorted beads or pearls
Two 2½"-long headpins
4" length of French wire
One set of earwires
Needlepoint pliers

Directions

1. Slide beads in place on one headpin. Bend headpin into desired shape.

2. Cut French wire in half. Slide one half onto headpin, allowing ⅜" of headpin to show. Repeat.

3. Form loop around earwire, using needlepoint pliers. Repeat.

❀ *Vivé la France* ❀ *Vivé la France* ❀ *Vivé la France* ❀ *Vivé la France* ❀

Coveted Crystals ✦ *Coveted Crystals* ✦ *Coveted Crystals* ✦ *Coveted Crystals* ✦

Coveted Crystals
N E C K L A C E

Materials

Approximately 1100 crystal AB 11/0
    seed beads
#2 silver-lined bugle beads:
    108 crystal
    120 pale amethyst
    72 lt. aqua
    72 sapphire blue
    84 pink
    40 med. green
    60 med. aqua
    84 lt. green
    84 med. purple
    72 dark red
    72 dark sapphire blue
    50 gold

Lamp beads:
    2 dark green 8mm round
    2 pink 12mm x 16mm long
      diamond
    2 dark blue 10mm round
    2 purple/blue 16mm x 30mm long
      diamond
    2 dark green 12mm round
    2 pink 16mm x 30mm long
      diamond
    2 dark blue 14mm round
    1 green/purple 16mm x 30mm long
      diamond
30 crystal 6/0 seed beads
24" length of ³⁄₈"-diameter clothesline
Weaving loom
Clasp and ring (see photo)

Directions

1. Following manufacturer's instructions, warp loom with lightweight nylon thread so warp threads are the length of one bugle bead apart.

2. Weave bugle beads and 11/0 seed beads according to Coveted Crystals Necklace Pattern. Note that each bugle bead is roughly equivalent to three seed beads. Work from END to CENTER, then repeat pattern backwards to END.

3. Join side of woven strip together around clothesline; see "Finishing a Tube" on page 122. Sew clasp on one end and ring on other.

4. Attach lamp beads; see Diagram 1 on page 85.

If you prefer, use different beads in place of the lamp beads. Choose beads of approximately the same color, size and shape, and attach them to the body of the necklace as shown in the instructions. Another variation would be to use large beads of the same color.

Coveted Crystals Necklace Pattern

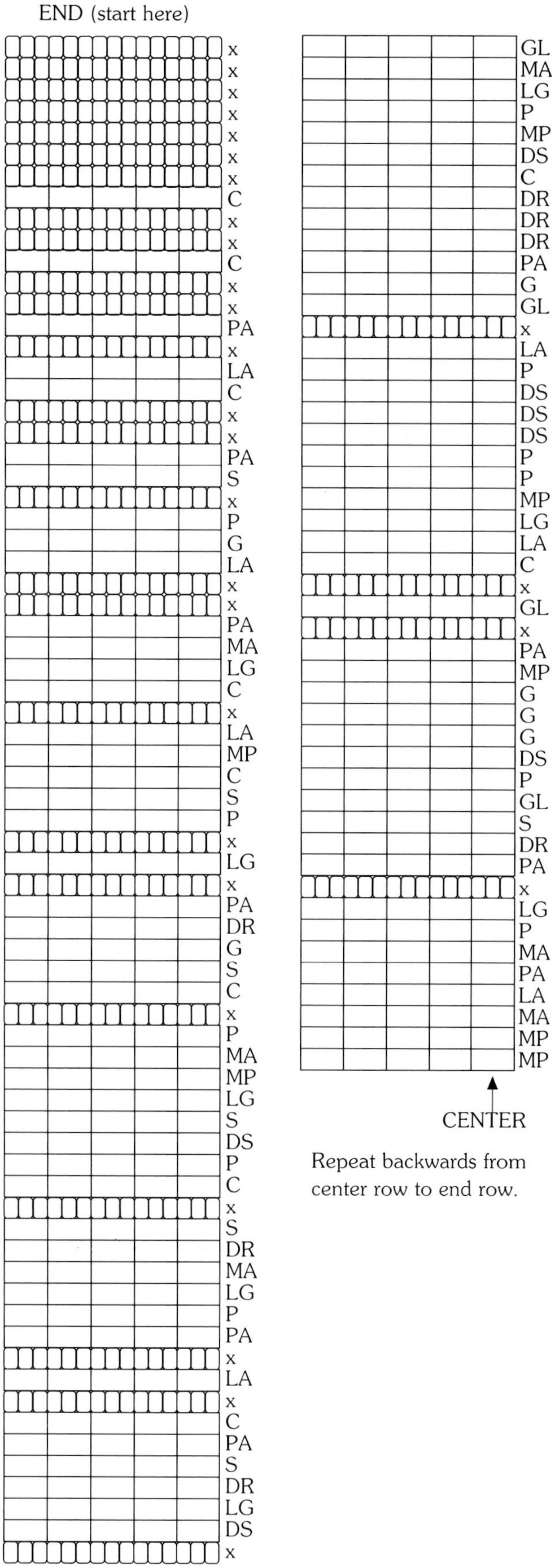
END (start here)
x
x
x
x
x
x
x
C
x
x
C
x
x
PA
x
LA
C
x
x
PA
S
x
P
G
LA
x
x
PA
MA
LG
C
x
LA
MP
C
S
P
x
LG
x
PA
DR
G
S
C
x
P
MA
MP
LG
S
DS
P
C
x
S
DR
MA
LG
P
PA
x
LA
x
C
PA
S
DR
LG
DS
x
GL
MA
LG
P
MP
DS
C
DR
DR
DR
PA
G
GL
x
LA
P
DS
DS
DS
P
P
MP
LG
LA
C
x
GL
x
PA
MP
G
G
G
DS
P
GL
S
DR
PA
x
LG
P
MA
PA
LA
MA
MP
MP
CENTER

Repeat backwards from center row to end row.

KEY

C	crystal
PA	pale amethyst
LA	lt. aqua
S	sapphire blue
P	pink
G	med. green
MA	med. aqua
LG	lt. green
MP	med. purple
DR	dark red
DS	dark sapphire
GL	gold
x	crystal AB seed beads 11/0

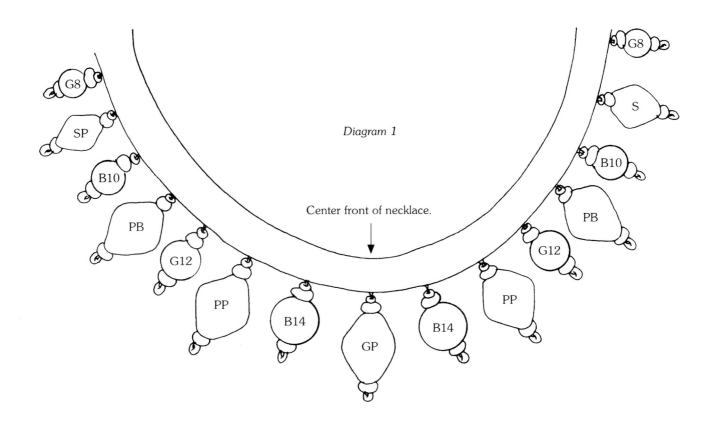

Diagram 1

Center front of necklace.

G8

SP

B10

PB

G12

PP

B14

GP

B14

PP

G12

PB

B10

S

G8

=== KEY ===

GP	green/purple 16mm x 30mm long diamond	PB	purple/blue 16mm x 30mm long diamond
B14	dark blue 14mm round	B10	dark blue 10mm round
PP	pink 16mm x 30mm long diamond	SP	pink 12mm x 16mm long diamond
G12	green 12mm round	G8	dark green 8mm round

❀ *Turquoise Twosome* ❀ *Turquoise Twosome* ❀ *Turquoise Twosome* ❀ *Turquoise Twosome* ❀

Turquoise Twosome

NECKLACE AND EARRINGS

Materials

One large turquoise bead (approximately 13mm x 22mm)

Two flat turquoise donuts (approximately 15mm diameter)

Two turquoise cylinders (approximately 13mm x 7mm)

Two flat turquoise disks (approximately 7mm diameter x 3mm deep)

Two 6mm round silver beads

Four 4mm round silver beads

Four 2mm round silver beads

Two sterling silver earwires

Two 1¾"-long silver headpins

One 26" length of black satin rattail cord

Sharp wirecutters

Round-nosed pliers

Glue

Directions

Necklace:

1. Thread large turquoise bead onto cord, placing it in center. Tie one knot on each side of bead.

2. Thread silver beads and make knots; see Diagram 1.

3. Tie knot at each end of remaining satin cord, leaving about ½" excess. Apply thin coat of clear glue to outside edge of knot. Let dry. Clip excess close to knot.

Earrings:

1. Thread beads onto headpin: see Diagram 2.

2. Clip excess headpin to ⅜" with wirecutters. Using the round-nosed pliers, form loop. Close headpin loop around earwire loop.

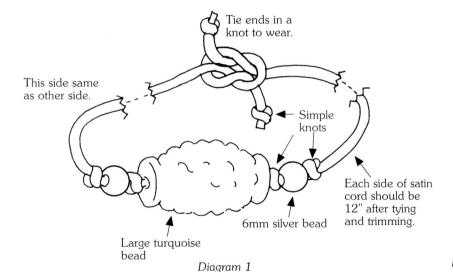

Tie ends in a knot to wear.

This side same as other side.

Simple knots

Each side of satin cord should be 12" after tying and trimming.

6mm silver bead

Large turquoise bead

Diagram 1

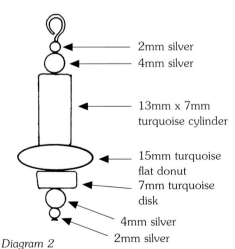

2mm silver
4mm silver

13mm x 7mm turquoise cylinder

15mm turquoise flat donut
7mm turquoise disk

4mm silver
2mm silver

Diagram 2

Scarab
PIN

Materials

Ten 4-4.5mm freshwater pearls
44 matte amethyst #2 bugle beads
100 opaque aqua 8/0 seed beads
20 opaque lavender 8/0 seed beads
16 matte amethyst 6/0 seed beads
2 lt. amethyst 6mm fire-polish crystals
100 lt. lavender in any of the
    following:
    delica, 13/0, 14/0, 12/0 3-cut

Approximately 350 metallic gold 12/0
    3-cut beads
One decorative 13mm x 18mm scarab
    or cabochon
4" x 6" bead card
4" x 6" backing fabric piece
Two 4" x 6" pieces of fusible webbing
Pinback

Directions

1. Transfer Scarab Pin Pattern to bead card. See "Patterns" on page 105.

2. Sew on all 8/0 beads.

3. Sew on bugle beads.

4. Sew on freshwater pearls, crystals, and 6/0 beads anchored with metallic gold 12/0 3-cut.

5. Fill border area with lt. lavender according to pattern.

6. Fill background and border with metallic gold 12/0 3-cut according to pattern.

7. Fuse backing fabric to stitched bead card. See "Fusing" on page 106.

8. Carefully trim excess card/fabric from edges.

9. Attach scarab or cabochon.

10. Attach to pinback.

Scarab Pin Pattern

KEY

O individual 8/0 opaque aqua anchored with gold 3-cuts

⊸ individual bugle beads

(P) freshwater pearls

—— lines of gold 12/0 3-cuts

━━ lines of opaque aqua 8/0

⌒ lines of opaque lavender 8/0

◯ matte amethyst 6/0 anchored with gold 3/-cut

S placement for scarab or cabochon

· fill with lt. lavender

✕ fill with metallic gold 3-cut

⬡ crystals

❋ *Silver Star* ❋ *Silver Star* ❋ *Silver Star* ❋ *Silver Star* ❋ *Silver Star* ❋ *Silver Star* ❋

Silver Star
CHOKER

Materials

Four small silver beads
Four large silver beads
Two large silver decorated beads
54 twisted silver ¼" tubes
One 16" length of light tigertail cord

One silver clasp
Two silver crimps
One silver charm
One silver jump ring

Directions

1. Attach one side of clasp to one end of tigertail with a crimp; see "Finishing Strands" on page 103. Flatten crimp until tigertail is secure.

2. Thread 27 twisted silver tubes onto tigertail. Add one small silver bead, one large silver bead, one decorated bead, one large silver bead, one small silver bead and star charm. Repeat in reverse.

3. Attach other side of clasp to tigertail, using a crimp. Remove any slack in tigertail before crimping. Trim excess.

4. Attach silver jump ring.

Victoria's Legacy
PIN

Materials

13/0 seed beads:
  23 lustered med. purple
  70 lustered med. green
  44 lustered orchid
  28 lustered lt. green
  68 lustered rose
  35 lustered cream
  250 iris blue

2" x 3" piece of 18-count needlepoint canvas
2" x 3" piece of fusible webbing
Sterling-silver pinback (see photo)
Glue
Iron

Direction

1. Stitch design; see Victoria's Legacy Pin Pattern. See "Beading on Needlepoint Canvas" on page 110.

2. With beaded side down on ironing board, use a burst of steam to infuse the canvas with heat. Quickly adjust so canvas is square.

3. With paper side up, place fusible webbing over back of canvas. Place piece of clean white paper over webbing. Iron for five seconds. Let cool.

4. Attach to pinback.

Victoria's Legacy Pin Pattern

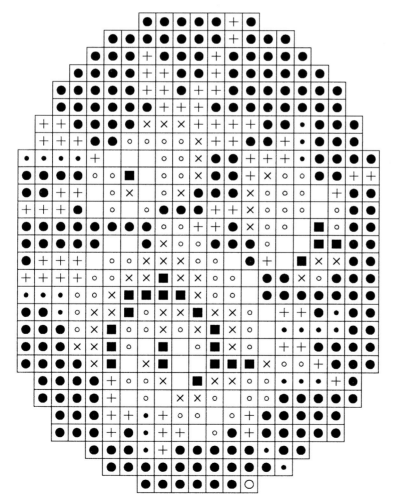

=== KEY ===

■ lustered med. purple

● iris blue

+ lustered med. green

✕ lustered orchid

• lustered lt. green

○ lustered rose

☐ lustered cream

⊛ *Gold & Silver* ⊛ *Gold & Silver* ⊛ *Gold & Silver* ⊛ *Gold & Silver* ⊛ *Gold & Silver* ⊛

Gold & Silver
C A P   E A R R I N G S

Materials

600 silver-lined crystal 14/0 seed beads
200 silver-lined gold 14/0 seed beads
110 silver-lined root beer 14/0 seed beads
22 half-silvered 4mm English cut beads
40 silver-lined gold 11/0 seed beads

Two gold-finished earwires
Two 7mm-diameter gold-finished end caps
Two 1" eyepins
Lightweight nylon thread

Directions

1. Make eleven strands for each earring; see Diagram 1. Leave doubled thread end for knotting about 3" longer than strand.

2. Gather strands into two bunches and tie together with one knot very near top of beads.

3. Attach end caps. See "Finishing Techniques" on page 102.

KEY

⬭ silver-lined crystal 14/0

⊕ silver-lined gold 14/0

⊡ silver-lined root beer 14/0

⬡ 4mm English cuts half-silver crystal

⬭ silver-lined gold 11/0

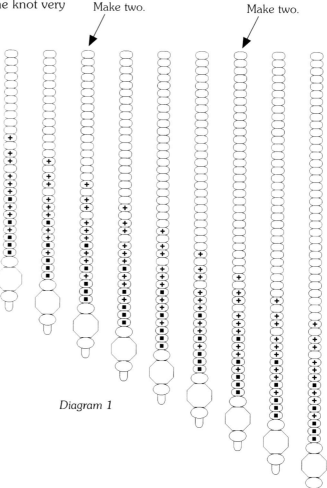

Make two.   Make two.

Diagram 1

Over the Peyote Rainbow
BRACELET

Materials

11/0 seed beads (per repeat):
- 64 black opaque
- 48 metallic gold
- 32 orchid opaque
- 44 green opaque
- 32 rose opaque
- 32 lt. orange opaque
- 32 lt. blue opaque
- 28 yellow opaque
- 32 aqua opaque

One 10" length of ⅜"-diameter
  clothesline
Neutral thread
Masking tape

Directions

1. Weave pattern according to Over the Peyote Rainbow Pattern; see "Peyote Stitch" on page 118.

2. Repeat pattern five times for an adult-sized bracelet, four times for a child-sized bracelet.

3. Cut clothesline ¾" longer than beadwork. Join edges of woven strip around clothesline, matching rows; see "Finishing a Tube" on page 122.

4. When about ¾" of joining is completed, stitch ends of clothesline together to form a loop; see Diagram 1. Wrap masking tape around joint; see Diagram 2.

5. Complete joining of sides. Work last woven row into first woven row and stitch together. Bury thread in weave. Clip excess.

Over the Peyote Rainbow Pattern

Seed beads needed per repeat.

- 64 black opaque
- 48 metallic gold
- 32 orchid opaque
- 44 green opaque
- 32 rose opaque
- 32 lt. orange opaque
- 32 lt. blue opaque
- 28 yellow opaque
- 32 aqua opaque

- - - - last row of pattern
first row of repeat
(same as top of pattern)

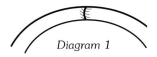

Diagram 1

Wrap tape carefully so there are no wrinkles. The tape serves only to smooth the stitched joint, not to hold it together.

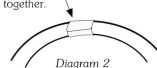

Diagram 2

❀ *Sunburst* ❀ *Sunburst* ❀ *Sunburst* ❀ *Sunburst* ❀ *Sunburst* ❀ *Sunburst* ❀

Sunburst
NECKLACE AND EARRINGS

Materials

One large central medallion with back loop in matte gold finish (approximately 2" diameter)

Approximately 90 matte gold finish 6/0 seed beads

Approximately 400 gold-finish 11/0 seed beads

Assortment of different-shaped, matte finished glass beads in sizes from 4mm to 12mm

Ten 2" gold-finish headpins, .021 gauge
One matte gold finish toggle clasp
Two gold finish crimps
Two matte gold finish ear findings with bottom loops
24" length of tigertail

Directions

Necklace:

1. Thread a 2" section of matte gold 11/0 onto tigertail and center it. Slip central medallion onto tigertail so it rests centered in the 2" section of 11/0 seed beads.

2. Thread remaining beads; see Sunburst Pattern.

3. Attach both sides of toggle clasp with crimp beads. Trim excess tigertail.

4. Make two dangles each of the following lengths: 1¾", 1½", 1¼", and 1".

Trim excess headpin to ⅜" on each dangle. Form a loop and attach dangles around necklace foundation where indicated. Curve headpins slightly so they hang toward center of necklace.

Earrings:

1. Thread one headpin with one 11/0, one 6/0, three larger beads, one 6/0 and one 11/0. Trim excess headpin to ⅜" and form a loop around bottom loop in ear finding. Close loop securely. Repeat for second earring.

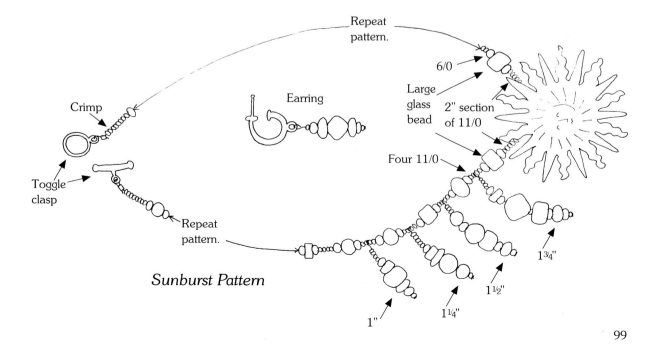

Sunburst Pattern

Repeat pattern.

Crimp

Toggle clasp

Repeat pattern.

Earring

6/0

Large glass bead

2" section of 11/0

Four 11/0

1¾"

1½"

1¼"

1"

Assorted Brick Stitch Designs

General Instructions

To help you in your creative efforts, every technique, piece of equipment, and hint you'll need to make this book's projects are here in these general instructions. You need to finish a tube? Look on page 122. Wonder how to make a Peyote stitch? See page 118. Want to make an attractive clasp? Go to page 124. Just remember, if you're stumped at some point, always return to these general instructions—everything you need is here!

Tools

Successful beadwork requires very few tools. A good assortment of needles is essential; sharp scissors are a must. Wire cutters, round-nosed and needlenose pliers are necessary for making earrings with headpins and eyepins. A good adjustable beading loom is a joy when making a long item, such as a belt or strap.

Shown are the different tools you'll need to do your bead-work. They include needles, scissors, wire cutters, round-nosed pliers, and needle-nose pliers.

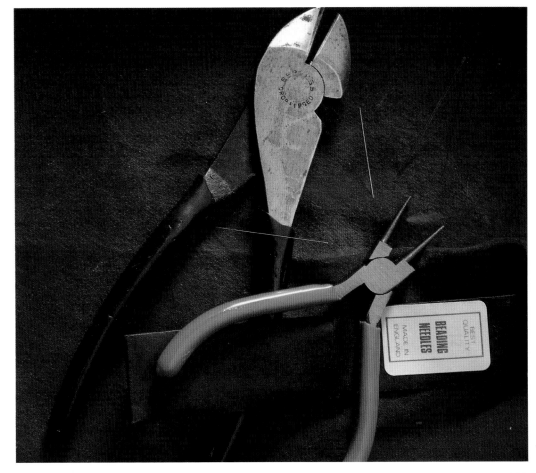

Even the most beautiful beads are diminished when poorly presented. The difference between a breathtaking necklace and one that looks rather shabby may only be a matter of the method used for stringing the beads.

The following are simple techniques that can change the outcome of your work dramatically without really complicating the procedure.

Choosing a Fiber: Use a fiber of an appropriate weight. For example, very heavy beads must be strung on a substantial fiber, such as heavy nylon, perle cotton or multi-filament rayon. Nylon filament similar to fishing line is also a good choice for projects with a good deal of weight.

Consider the way you want your necklace to drape when choosing a fiber. If you want the necklace to move freely, light silk or nylon, perhaps doubled for strength, is a good choice. But if you want the necklace

to take on a defined shape, or to curve predictably, you should use tigertail (lightweight twisted wire) or nylon filament (fishing line).

Bead Spacing and Knotting: Space the beads slightly apart so that each can be shown to its best advantage. One good method is to place a very small bead between each of the larger beads. This is particularly effective when stringing freshwater pearls, which tend to twist unattractively because of their irregular shape.

Knotting is another good method of spacing beads slightly apart. Simply make a knot in the fiber between beads. This is recommended for any glass beads that might be damaged by contact with adjacent beads. For example, crystals strung unknotted soon lose some of their sparkle because the glass surfaces rub together. They can also be annoyingly loud to wear; knots prevent the little grating noises that occur when crystal rubs against itself.

Shown are different fibers used in creating beadwork. They include tigertail, paper cord, leather cord, nylon thread, silk thread, rayon fiber, satin cord and metal wire.

Finishing Strands: The following are several methods of finishing your beaded strands:

⊛ Cover a final knot with cylindrical or conical bead caps by joining several strands of beads together; see Diagrams A and B.

⊛ Finish knotted strands with one big knot (knotted over itself until it is of substantial size). Then sew with matching thread to an attractive clasp; see Diagram C.

⊛ Knot nylon filament or nylon thread into a bead cap, then attach with a jump ring to a clasp; see Diagram D.

⊛ Secure tigertail to a jump ring or clasp with a crimp bead, which is squeezed tightly over the trimmed end to form a strong loop; see Diagrams E and F.

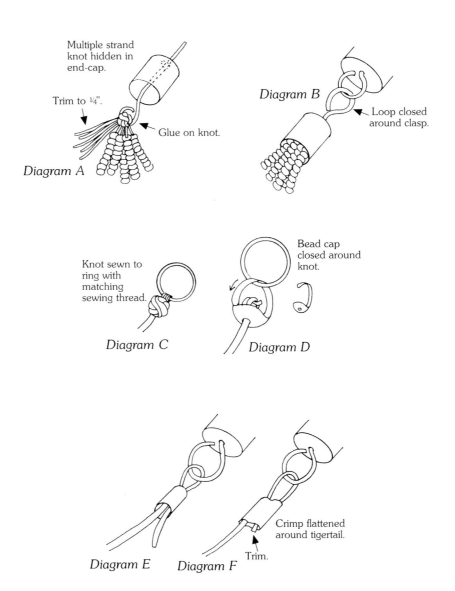

Multiple strand knot hidden in end-cap.

Trim to ¼".

Glue on knot.

Diagram A

Diagram B

Loop closed around clasp.

Knot sewn to ring with matching sewing thread.

Diagram C

Bead cap closed around knot.

Diagram D

Diagram E

Diagram F

Crimp flattened around tigertail.

Trim.

Removing Unwanted Beads

If you accidentally sew on the wrong color or a misshapen bead, or if your work is puckering, remove the offending bead by breaking it off with needlenose pliers. Close your eyes and look away as the bead breaks.

Bead Handling Tips

Who spilled the beads? There's no use crying over spilled beads. Instead, put a new bag in your vacuum cleaner and and vacuum them up. If only a few beads spilled, wet the tip of your finger to pick them up.

They're all wet! A moistened paper towel, wrung out a little, reduces the static electricity that builds up around glass beads. Place the wet towel on your flat container while working.

Mexican jumping beads! If you store your beads in a plastic bag, they will probably try to jump out when you open it. Blow into the bag lightly and the moisture from your breath will settle the beads enough to pour them out.

Temptation! It is very tempting when weaving to loop away without recounting your beads after threading on a very long row—but you will only do this once. If you have to rip out a row, first, pull the needle off the thread. Then, use the tip of the needle to gently pull the thread out of the beads.

Organization. Sort beads and place them in small containers with flat, small-lipped lids. A muffin tin also comes in handy as a useful organizer.

Thread Hints

Soaping or waxing the thread keeps it from tangling. Run the thread across the surface of the soap or wax, then pull the thread between your fingertips to remove any excess.

Beading on Surfaces

Getting Started

Beads can be sewn onto almost any surface, such as fabric, leather, and paper (card weight); each of these materials has special properties, but the technique used to sew on beads is the same. The only difference is the needle and thread you choose.

Leather should be lightweight and easily needled. It requires a very sharp, strong needle if the leather is too stiff to push the needle; therefore, ordinary beading needles are not a good choice. Try using a #10 quilting needle and ordinary sewing thread.

If the leather is still too stiff to push the needle through easily, bead your design onto card or fabric first, then apply a layer of fusible webbing (hot melt sheet adhesive) to the back of the work. Fuse the beadwork to the leather, then secure it with additional small stitches. Be aware that leather can stretch easily and the stretching is not easily corrected. If your leather is so light that it will not hold its shape, iron on a layer of lightweight fusible interfacing (such as Pellon® fusible featherweight) to help the leather maintain its shape.

Heavy fabrics such as felt or closely-woven cottons will probably not need any special treatment. Use a #9 embroidery needle or a #10 quilting needle.

Lightweight fabrics such as silk and rayon need to be supported. If the fabric is not sheer, a good backing is lightweight felt fused directly to the fabric. If the fabric is sheer, you may need to support it with another layer of sheer fabric or simply double the fabric you are using. A regular beading needle is sufficient for these fabrics. When beading on card stock, a #9 embroidery needle or a #10 quilting needle works well along with ordinary sewing thread.

Patterns

The method used to transfer the design onto the beading surface varies with the surface you choose. However, when using fabrics, always:

❀ Pre-shrink the fabric with a hot steam iron before transferring the design.

❀ Wash the fabric in a mild detergent to ensure the fabric is not adversely affected.

❀ Use a graphite pencil to draw the design on the fabric. Transfer ink or pencil never washes out completely—it becomes part of the fabric's chemistry.

❀ Wash the piece with a mild detergent after completion to remove the graphite.

One way to transfer a pattern is to draw the pattern directly onto the surface. On lightweight fabrics, place the fabric over the design and trace the pattern using a light touch. This works especially well if you work on a transparent fabric with light coming from underneath, such as a glass-topped coffee table or a window pane tilted in.

Another method is to make a heat transfer using the pens or pencils available in some art or needlework stores. This works especially well with any fabric that has a high synthetic content, such as polyester, acrylic or felt.

Trace the design on tracing paper, then turn it face down and retrace it in the transfer pencil. Iron the design onto the fabric with a hot iron, holding the iron in each position for about 12 to 15 seconds. Please remember, because this method uses transfer pencil, not all of the lines will wash out.

A third method is to sew the lines onto the fabric. First trace the design on tracing paper. Next, place the fabric and paper together. Hand or machine sew the lines directly through the paper, then tear the paper away. This works well for lines, but is a poor choice for designs with lots of little embellishments.

When using card stock, the best method for transferring the design is to simply photocopy the page directly; since the authors and publishers of this book grant permission to photocopy, there is no violation of copyright law. You could also use the methods for fabrics described above.

Slipstitch

Slipstitch is an almost invisible stitch used to join edges. Using a single strand of thread knotted at one end, insert the needle at 1 and bring it out at 2, picking up a few threads; see Diagram G. Slide the needle under the folded edge of the fabric ¼" and catch it in the stitch.

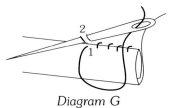

Diagram G

Couching

Couching is a sewing technique used to anchor objects to any surface. With thread, bring the needle up at 1, down at 2. Repeat to attach the entire length as desired; see Diagram H.

Diagram H

Fusing

To fuse backing fabric to beaded projects, you need a thick white towel; completed beadwork; glue; fusible webbing with paper removed; fabric; a sheet of clean, white paper; and an iron.

Layer and center the components; see Diagram I. Press the iron down flat for five seconds. Shift the iron and press for two seconds more to eliminate any steam holes. Allow the piece to cool completely. With nail scissors, trim excess card and fabric. Run a thin line of diluted white glue around entire outside edge to secure.

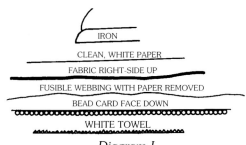

Diagram I

Sewing Seed Beads

For small areas and tight curves, it is best to sew on each bead individually. Poke a hole in the card with the needle in the desired location, and bring the thread from back to front. Slip the bead over the needle, and let it slide all the way down the thread until it rests on the card in the desired place. Bring the needle back through the surface right in the same hole or very close by so the bead is secured; see Diagram J.

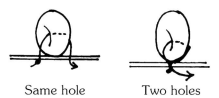

Same hole   Two holes

Diagram J

For gentle curves and outlines, seed beads may be sewn on two at a time; see Diagram K. Poke a hole through the surface about two bead lengths forward on the stitching line (hole A). Bring the needle up from back to front. Slip two beads on the needle, letting them slide all the way down the thread until they are on their round sides on the stitching line. Bring the needle down through the surface from front to back (hole B) so the two beads are secured. Poke another hole in the stitching line about two bead lengths forward (hole C). Bring the needle up from back to front and slip on two more beads. Slide them to the surface, and bring the needle from front to back in the first hole made (hole A). Repeat these steps for the length of the line.

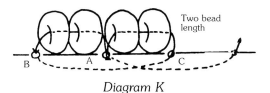

Diagram K

Backtracking

After completing a line of seed beads, fortify the line with backtracking. Bring the needle up just past the last bead in the line, and run the thread back through all beads in the line. Just after the last bead, bring the needle to the back of the surface you're sewing on, and secure the thread. This is especially important for outlines around the outside edge of a design. If the beads being backtracked have very fine holes, it may be necessary to use a #10 needle. It will help to run through only three beads at a time, particularly if the line is curved. Keep running through until all beads in one line are joined together by a single thread; see Diagram L. Tighten it until the line is smooth and neat, but not so tight that there is puckering.

Backtracking thread

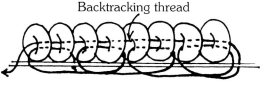

Diagram L

For filling large areas, you may sew several beads at one time, provided they are anchored with small stitches along the length of the line (similar to the needlecraft technique known as couching). Bring the needle up at your chosen starting place and slip on several beads, laying them against the surface to see if they fill the desired space comfortably; see Diagram M.

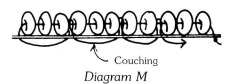

Couching

Diagram M

Small gaps in the beads will not be noticeable, but large gaps and puckering will not be attractive in the finished work. Try to space the beads so they touch each other gently, but are not crowded. Cramming six beads into a five-bead length will be far more noticeable than the tiny gaps that naturally occur between the rounded edges of beads sewn close to each other.

Bugle beads are almost always sewn on individually. Place the unsewn bugle bead on the surface in approximately the desired placement and poke a hole at one end. Bring the needle from back to front in this hole, then slip on the bugle bead, allowing it to rest against the surface. Bring the needle to the back of the surface at the other end of the bead and pull until the bead rests firmly against the surface; see Diagram N.

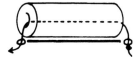

Diagram N

A long line of bugle beads placed end-to-end may be sewn on at one time, provided you anchor the line to the surface in several places; see Diagram O. You may want to backtrack the line to firm it up and stabilize it. Since some bugle beads have extremely

Diagram O

fine holes, you will probably need to use a #10 quilting needle to backtrack bugle

beads. You may have to run through each bead individually when backtracking.

Large bugle beads (#5 and longer) may be sewn on individually as just described. One concern when sewing on any bugle bead, but especially larger ones, is the possibility that the cut end of the glass tube will cut or fray your thread. This is one reason why you should never tighten the thread to the point of puckering.

When bugle beads are sewn in a fan-shaped area, there will be small gaps between them in some places; see Diagram P. Ignore these spaces, as they will not be particularly noticeable in your finished piece. If they are truly bothersome to you, lightly paint on a thin wash of pale gray watercolor using a small brush. This softens the appearance of the surface between the beads.

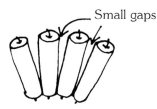

Small gaps

Diagram P

Crystals are sewn on so one of the cut facets lies flat against the card. Place the unsewn crystal in its desired position, and poke a hole through one end. Bring the needle up from back to front through this hole, and slip the crystal on, allowing it to rest against the surface in its final position. Bring the needle from front to back at the other end of the crystal; see Diagram Q. Very small crystals (4mm or 5mm) are essentially treated the same as seed beads. They are sewn on in lines and backtracked or sewn on individually, depending on the final position. Larger crystals (6mm to

12mm) require some additional treatment such as a cross-stitch. Stitch up from lower left, then slip on the crystal and bring the needle down through the card at the upper right. Secure the crystal by returning the thread through the crystal, lower right to upper left; see Diagram R.

Since there will be some thread visible at each end of the crystal, you may choose to slip on one or two small seed beads prior to slipping on the crystal. Then use one or two small seed beads at the other end of the thread as well; see Diagram S.

Diagram Q

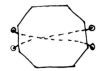

Diagram R

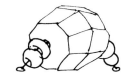

Diagram S

Sewing Freshwater Pearls

Pearls have extremely fine holes, and you will have to use a #10 quilting needle. Check each pearl to see that it slips over the needle before marking the surface for it. Position it unsewn on the surface as desired, and poke a hole at one end. Bring the needle up from back to front, then slip the pearl on, allowing it to rest on the surface; see Diagram T. Note that most freshwater pearls have one side that is slightly flattened. This side should be touching the surface and the attractive, rounded surface should face up. It is nearly impossible to backtrack all freshwater pearls. If they are used in a continuous line, sew them on carefully to insure an attractive appearance.

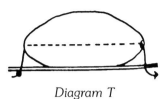

Diagram T

Sewing Semi-Precious Chips

Most semi-precious chips are drilled through the short side. Position the chip as desired unsewn on the surface. Push the needle through its hole, poking a hole in the surface below. Bring the needle from back to front in this hole and slip the chip over the needle until it rests flat against the surface. Slide one small seed bead over the needle, then insert the needle back through the chip hole. Pull it tight until the small seed bead acts as an anchor on the top surface of the chip; see Diagram U.

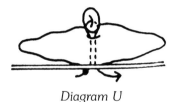

Diagram U

Sewing Odd-Shaped Beads

In general, the shape of the bead determines which method of sewing is best. If a bead is donut-shaped, it probably is best sewn using the technique used for semi-precious chips. Long, narrow beads are treated in a similar manner to bugle beads. Faceted or large round beads are sewn on much like faceted crystals. Below are examples of how to deal with odd beads; see Diagram V.

Diagram V

Beading on Needlepoint Canvas

Beads are sewn individually to the intersection of two canvas threads, just as in regular needlepoint, where one stitch is formed over the intersection of two canvas threads. The appearance of the finished work is quite similar to needlepoint, because each oblong oval bead is approximately the same size and shape as a traditional half-cross stitch. Shown are examples of a Short Backstitch and a Long Backstitch; see Diagrams W and X.

Experienced needlepointers will initially balk, however, at running the thread in a different direction. In order to make the bead slant to the right, the thread must slant to the left. Additionally, a beading or fine embroidery needle must be used, which will feel very tiny to a stitcher accustomed to the firm bulk of a tapestry needle.

Here are some rules for beading on needlepoint canvas:

⊕ Use Interlock (single thread lock-weave) canvas or Penelope (double threaded canvas). Mono (single thread overweave) canvas is too unstable for use with beads.

⊕ Use a #9 embroidery needle or a #10 quilting needle. They are shorter than most beading needles and will be easier to handle.

⊕ Use doubled ordinary sewing thread matched to the color of the canvas. If you are beading on a painted canvas and do not wish to keep an assortment of threads around to match your colors, use a neutral medium gray.

⊕ Count one horizontal row a time. It is far easier to do this than to wander all around the canvas as you work. Mark off each row after completion; it will help you keep track of your place.

⊕ Use 11/0 seed beads on 14-count canvas; use 14/0 seed beads on 18-count canvas.

⊕ Paint the design on the canvas before beading, if possible, following your stitching chart.

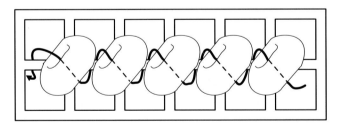

Diagram W
Short Backstitch

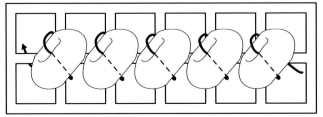

Diagram X
Long Backstitch

Stitching Needlepoint

The Beaded Bouquet Clutch Bag combines beadwork with traditional needlepoint. The following are the needlepoint instructions you'll need to complete the designs. First, separate one ply from the Persian wool and use two plies at a time. Reserve the removed ply for later recombination with another removed ply of the same color.

Begin by holding one inch of yarn on the back of the canvas, then catching it in your first few stitches until it is secure. Trim excess later. Bring the needle up from back to front of the canvas at odd numbers and down from front to back at even numbers. When the strand is ended, secure the yarn on the back of the canvas by running it under several stitches until it is secure. Trim excess.

Basketweave Stitch: Basketweave stitch is worked in diagonal rows; see Diagram XX. Begin in the northeast corner of a color area and progress in diagonal rows toward the southwest. The canvas does not need to be turned. This stitch is preferable to continental because it causes less distortion of the canvas.

Continental Stitch: Continental stitch is worked in horizontal rows from right to left (unless you are left-handed, in which case you follow the directions backwards); see Diagram Y. At the end of the row, the work is turned and the stitching progresses from right to left again. Work in this back-and-forth pattern until the color selection is complete. This stitch distorts the canvas quite a bit, so use it only where basketweave cannot be used.

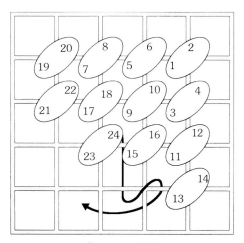

Diagram XX
Basketweave Stitch

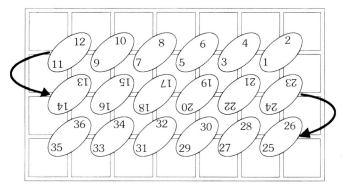

Diagram Y
Continental Stitch

1. Trim excess to ¼". Notch corners and outside curves. Clip inside curves; *see Diagram Z.*

2. Press trimmed edges down flat against back of work; *see Diagram AA.*

3. Use trimmed, pressed piece as a template to cut lining, adding ¼" to all edges; *see Diagram BB.* Trim and press lining as in Step 1.

4. Use matching thread and tiny stitches to slipstitch lining to back of canvas; *see Diagram CC.*

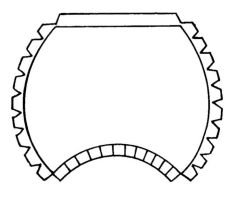

Diagram Z

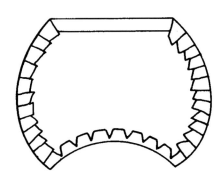

Diagram AA

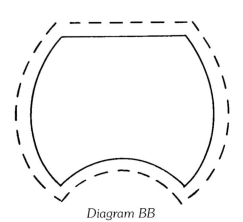

Diagram BB

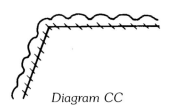

Diagram CC

Backings for Odd-Shaped Pieces

1. Use finished design piece to cut lining, backing and interfacing, adding ¼" to all edges; see Diagram DD. (Use felt if more stiffness is desired.)

2. Layer lining right side up, backing right side down, and interfacing. Baste with loose stitches; see Diagram EE.

3. Sew all edges, leaving an opening for turning; see Diagram FF.

4. Trim interfacing to the seam line. Notch corners and curves of lining and backing. Turn right side out. Press edges flat. Slipstitch opening; see Diagram GG.

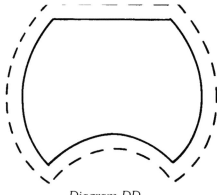

Diagram DD

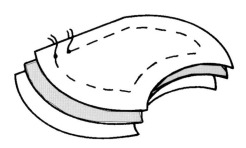

Diagram EE

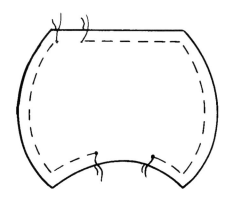

Diagram FF

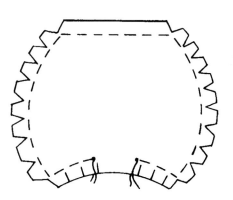

Diagram GG

Bead Needleweaving

Bead needleweaving may remind you of crocheting. The first row is worked, then subsequent rows are looped into the first row in a predictable way. Unlike crochet, which is usually worked from written directions, bead needleweaving is worked from a gridded pattern (except when weaving a sphere, which is worked from written directions).

Vertical rows of counted beads are attached to the previous vertical rows by a series of evenly spaced loops. The ideal pattern is to loop after every third bead. In some cases, where great strength is needed, you may want to loop more frequently.

The first few rows are somewhat unstable and may seem difficult to work. Tricks for dealing with this temporary instability are described on the following pages. Be patient! After two or three rows, the weaving will be quite easy to handle. Before you know it, you will have discovered the magic of "beauty and the beads."

Needles: Because of their great length, traditional beading needles are not well suited for needleweaving. A #9 embroidery needle is ideal when working with seed beads size 11 or larger. For some finely drilled stones and pearls, a #10 quilting needle is recommended.

Thread types: *Ordinary mercerized cotton sewing thread* is recommended for most needleweaving. Choose a neutral color that is similar in theme to your bead design. It is nearly impossible to weave without a little thread showing between the beads, so try to minimize the distraction by using compatible thread.

Light nylon can be used, but it has greater bulk than ordinary sewing thread and should be used only when strength is a consideration. If you are using a lot of valuable stones or your beadweaving piece is supporting any weight, nylon is a good choice.

Fine silk or cotton embroidery floss is a good choice for use in needleweaving. Separate the plies of cotton 6-ply embroidery floss and use only one ply at a time.

Metallic threads are not recommended because the surface fiber tends to fray and ravel. When pulling metallic thread through a tight-fitting bead, fibers bunch up around the bead opening.

Adding a New Thread

When about 3" of thread remains unbeaded on the needle, it is time to add a new thread. Remove the needle from the old thread and cut a new 30" length. A longer piece tends to tangle, and a shorter piece requires frequent additions of thread.

Tie a square knot so that the knot lands about 1" from where the old thread emerges from the beadwork; see Diagram HH. Place a tiny dot of glue on the knot. Wipe off any excess glue, but you don't need to wait for the glue to dry before proceeding.

Continue beading as if you were using one continuous thread. Let the thread ends protrude from the work until the new thread is well established within the weave; see Diagram II. Then pull gently on the ends and clip them close so they disappear into the weave. You may find it necessary to use a smaller needle until you have passed the area of the knot.

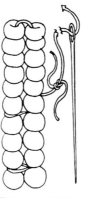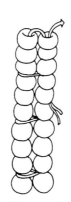

Diagram HH   Diagram II

Squared Needleweaving

In these instructions, the vertical rows are numbered from left to right. Row 1 is leftmost for a right-handed person. A left-handed person should start with the highest-numbered row and work right to left.

The work always proceeds in the direction of your dominant hand. The beads of each row are numbered from 1, beginning at the top of each vertical row and increasing to the bottom of the row. The diagrams show a 12-bead row; see Diagram JJ on page 116.

To begin, make a "stopper bead," which keeps the design pattern beads from slipping off the needle; see Diagram JJ. Cut a length of thread about 30" long and thread a needle so that a 5" tail remains. A longer thread tends to tangle, and a

shorter thread necessitates frequent re-threadings.

Slip one bead of any color over the needle, and position it about 3" from the long end of the thread. Loop the thread back through the bead and pull it tightly. Secure the stopper bead to a flat or slightly curved surface to stabilize the thread. Some suggestions are a tabletop, the arm of a chair, or a small cushion. Remove the stopper bead after the first few rows.

Thread the beads of row 1 from top to bottom; see diagram JJ. Skip the last bead threaded, inserting the needle back through all the beads on the thread. The needle should emerge from the top bead of row 1.

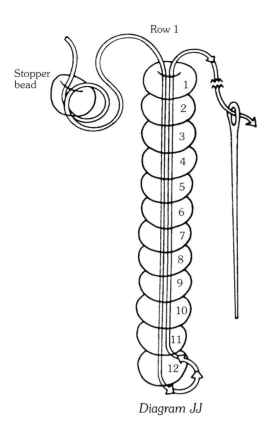

Row 1

Stopper bead

1
2
3
4
5
6
7
8
9
10
11
12

Diagram JJ

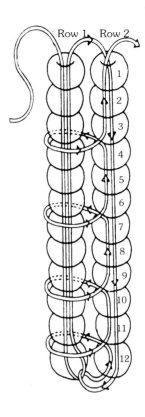

Row 1   Row 2

1
2
3
4
5
6
7
8
9
10
11
12

Diagram KK

Draw a line through the first vertical row of the chart to show it has been completed. Thread the beads of row 2, again reading from top to bottom; see Diagram KK. Always recount the beads against the pattern to be sure they are in order.

Insert the needle into the loop exposed at the bottom of row 1. Pull the thread gently until the whole second row is taut but not tight. It should rest against the first row without much puckering.

Insert the needle into the last bead of row 2 (bead 12) and bring the thread out until it is taught but not tight. Loop the thread around row 1 so it nestles in the space between beads 12 and 11 of row 2, bringing the needle out in the space between beads 10 and 9 on row 2. Again, the thread should be taut, but not tight.

Loop the thread around row 1 so it nestles in the space between beads 10 and 9 of row 1. Insert the needle into the next three beads on row 2 (beads 9, 8 and 7) and bring the needle out in the space between beads 7 and 6 on row 2.

Tighten the thread again, then loop it around the first row so it nestles in the space between beads 7 and 6 on row 1. Insert the needle into the next three beads on row 2 (beads 6, 5 and 4) and repeat the looping/inserting process until the thread emerges from bead 1 of row 2. After row 2, you may no longer need to stabilize the work. It gets easier and easier to handle as the weaving grows.

All subsequent rows are worked the same, except that the first loop (nestled between beads 12 and 11 on row 1) is not made. It is added to the first row to stabilize the work, but is not especially needed in the following rows. The pattern of loops may be worked in any way. If you wish to make a loop between every beads, you may do so, but a three-bead repeat is most effective for needleweaving. The more frequently you loop, the stiffer the woven piece.

Row 1 Row 2 Row 3

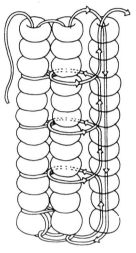

Diagram LL

And beyond

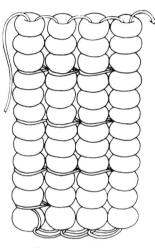

Diagram MM

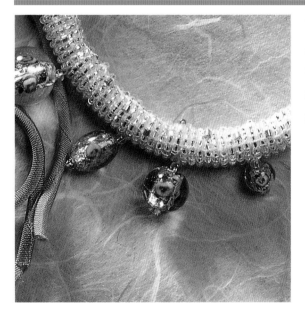

The Mille Fleur bracelet on page 30 uses the squared needleweaving technique.

Peyote Stitch

Peyote stitch differs from both squared needleweaving and loom weaving in that its pattern is diagonal. The resulting weaving is quite sturdy, but extremely flexible. First, thread the beads of rows one and two; see Diagram NN.

Next, add the beads of row 3, working them into the beads of row 2. Pull thread slightly to arrange beads so that there a is little slack, but the rows do not pucker; see Diagram OO.

Finally, add the beads of row 4 worked into the beads of row 3. Pull to take up slack slightly. Continue until all of the rows are beaded; see Diagram PP.

Ordinary sewing thread is a good choice for weaving the peyote stitch. A short, very fine needle (such as a #10 quilting needle) works well; there can be quite a thread build-up inside the beads and the needle must be quite small in consideration of this. Peyote Weave designs made from square beads such as Delicas or Antiques will not have as much flexibility as those made with ordinary seed beads.

Peyote Stitch weaves can be wrapped around shaped objects, stretched, twisted and otherwise manipulated for some very interesting effects. The weave can be made using a single-bead or double-bead pattern. Patterns are shown in grid form, and each row is worked in the opposite direction from the previous row.

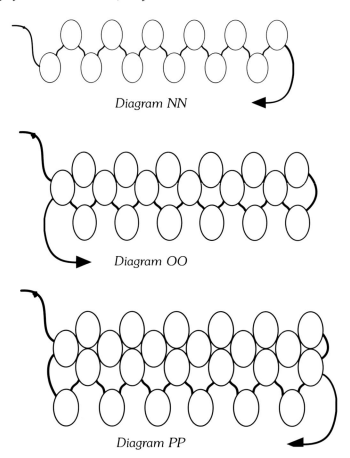

Diagram NN

Diagram OO

Diagram PP

Brick Stitch

Brick stitch is a diagonal weaving technique in which the beads lay against one another like alternating bricks. All work progresses outward from a foundation row. Each new row is looped into the previous row one bead at a time. The resulting weave is strong and flexible, and can be used for many different purposes.

The foundation row is worked with two needles. Cut a length of thread about 24" long and thread each end onto a needle. Center the first bead of the foundation row between the two needles, then form the foundation row; see Diagram QQ.

Thereafter, you will work with one needle at a time. It's convenient to remove the needle from the thread end not currently in use as it minimizes the tangling of the two threads; see Diagrams RR and SS.

Brick stitch is wonderful for making beaded earrings. Since it is quite easy to make diamond-shaped patterns in brick stitch, it is frequently used in earrings where one pointed end is sewn onto an earfinding with a loop. Samples of different brick stitch designs are provided on page 100.

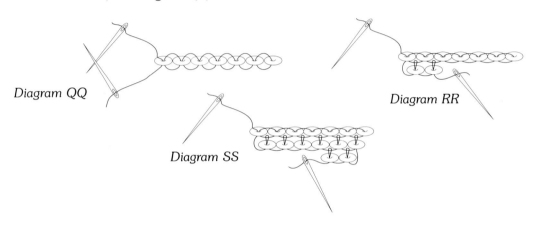

Diagram QQ

Diagram SS

Diagram RR

Examples of Brick stitch.

Looming

Looming produces a strong, uniform piece of woven beadwork. Of all the weaving techniques, looming progresses the quickest; it is an easy technique to master, and there is an abundance of designs available for use with looms ; see Diagram TT.

Most bead looms come with very good directions for use. If you've inherited one without its original carton, however, here are some simple guidelines for looming:

⊛ When threading on the warp (vertical loom threads), allow about 5" of extra thread on each end of the planned work to allow for later finishing.

⊛ Use a very long beading needle; if your work is not terribly wide, you can count an entire row at one time.

⊛ Tie on new threads at the beginning of the row, then dab a small amount of glue on the knot. Let the knot fall within the row, then clip off the protruding ends.

⊛ Use a lightweight but strong working thread. Nylon is a good choice for looming.

⊛ When weaving with bugle beads, thread on the warp so there is the length of 3 seed beads (11/0) between threads.

⊛ Try using a decorative warp such as dyed linen, perle cotton, or satin cord for a different look.

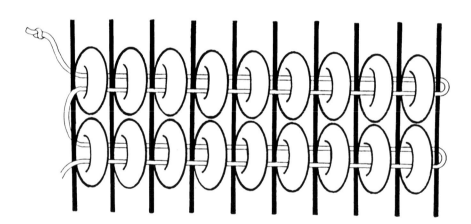

Diagram TT

Joining

When weaving a particularly large piece of beadwork, such as might be used in a purse or makeup case, it is easier to work small pieces and join them together; see Diagram UU. It is a good idea to use a very small needle for this procedure because the buildup of thread inside the bead holes can make it difficult to get a larger needle through. If you simply cannot get the needle through, skip the clogged bead and go on to the next row. It will not be noticeable in the finished piece.

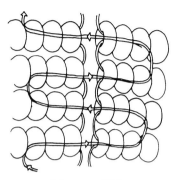

Diagram UU

Fringes

When designs with fringes are patterned, there is a separation between the sections that show the foundation pattern and the fringe pattern.

When forming fringes, the tension of the thread is important. Try to leave enough space so the fringes move freely, but not so much that there is a lot of visible thread. Part of the beauty of fringes is their motion; see Diagram VV. Lack of motion impedes the beauty of the overall design.

The three-bead end (also known as a "picot") is worked by skipping the last three beads and running the needle back through the remaining beads on the fringe. Don't pull too tightly, and try to settle the beads evenly at the end; see Diagram WW. Try using one color for the last four beads. It forms a diamond and gives an interesting dimension to the design.

The simple one-bead end finish is worked by skipping the last bead and running the needle back through the remaining beads on the fringe. Be sure to nestle the bead sideways for a neat appearance; see Diagram XX.

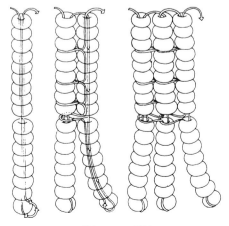

Diagram VV

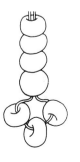

Diagram WW

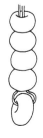

Diagram XX

Finishing a Tube

Finishing a tube is simply a matter of securing the woven beadwork neatly around the foundation material of your choice. Ordinary clothesline is a nice foundation for a three-dimensional tube.

After all weaving is completed, trim any excess threads that occur in the body of the weave. If there is a long piece of thread left at the end of the weave, use this to begin sewing the long edges together. Otherwise, bury a new thread within the weave at one end.

Cut a length of clothesline that will be at least 1" longer than the planned length of the tube. Wrap the woven length around the clothesline at the threaded end and weave the edges together. Line up the beads on one edge of the strip to the beads in the same row on the other edge of the strip; see Diagram YY.

Continue weaving back and forth until the entire length has been joined together. Trim the ends of the clothesline very closely to the end of the weave. It may be necessary to use a very small needle.

Finish the ends with seed beads that coordinate or complement the design of the piece you are finishing. Have the thread emerge from one of the beads on the outermost row of the weave on either end. Work rounds of beads according to the following instructions and Diagram ZZ.

Round 1. Work two beads into each group of three beads around the end. This reduces the number of beads on the round from 18 to 12.

Round 2. Work one bead into each group of two beads in the round of 12 beads. This reduces the number of beads from 12 to six.

Round 3. Run the thread through the remaining six beads and tighten it just so the gap closes. Do not pull it too tightly or the end will pucker. Bury the remaining thread in the weave (not the clothesline) and trim it.

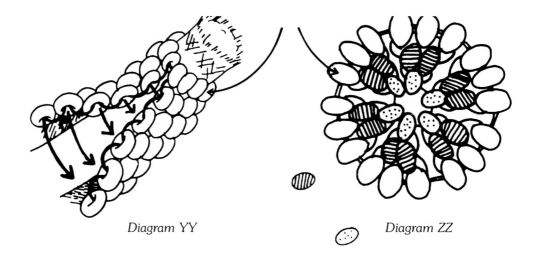

Diagram YY   *Diagram ZZ*

Attaching Backing

To finish the back of woven projects, you will need scissors, lightweight cardboard (such as a piece of cereal box), common pins, needle and thread, fabric that coordinates with beaded piece and tacky glue.

1. Lay the finished beadwork face down on the cardboard. Insert pins into the cardboard at the corners of the woven piece to mark the shape; see Diagram AAA.

2. Connect the dots, then cut the cardboard about ⅛" smaller all around than the marked shape; see Diagram BBB.

3. Using the cut cardboard as a guide, cut a piece of fabric with a margin of about ½" all around. Notch fabric at all corners; see Diagram CCC.

4. Center the cut cardboard shape on the fabric. Put several small dots of glue on the back of the fabric. Fold the edges of the fabric over the cardboard and glue the edges lightly; see Diagram DDD.

5. Position the fabric-covered cardboard on the back of the beadwork. Secure it to the beadwork with small invisible stitches; see Diagram EEE. When attaching a pinback or barrette, sew right through the cardboard, if possible.

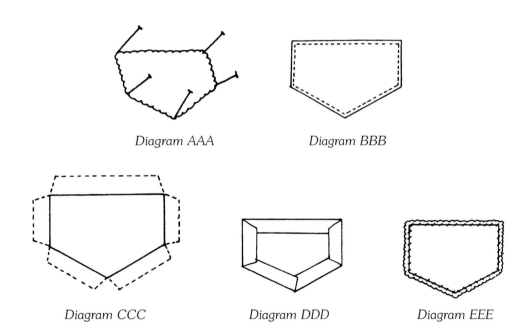

Diagram AAA   Diagram BBB

Diagram CCC   Diagram DDD   Diagram EEE

Other Crafty Ideas

Working with Leather Cord

Using leather cord as a foundation for a beaded necklace is so simple that you will almost feel guilty about it. The only complicating factor is that the holes on the beads you are using need to be large enough to accommodate the bulkiness of the cord. Wood, bone and metal beads tend to have larger holes than glass beads, and you can, of course, always make your own beads from clay or wood.

Before cutting your leather cord, you will need to decide which type of closure you will make for the necklace. There are two simple methods of closure: crimp with clasp, or bead with loop.

From the crimp with clasp, you do not need to allow any extra length for the finishing.

Simply thread on the desired beads, then pinch the crimp onto both trimmed ends of the leather cord. Open the loops on your clasp and then close them around the crimp loops; see Diagram FFF.

For the bead with loop closure, you will need to allow about 2½" extra beyond the desired length of the necklace. Use a 16-18mm bead. Form a loop in both ends of the leather (one end already having a bead on it) and wrap the loop closed; see Diagram GGG. You may choose almost any fiber or lightweight cord for wrapping. Prior to finishing the wrap, dab a dot of glue on the leather end so that the leather surfaces under the wrap are glued together. You should wrap before the glue dries.

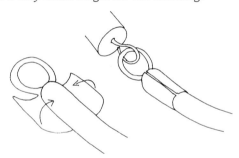

Diagram FFF

Diagram GGG

Leather cord finished with bead and loop.

A crimp clasp end.

Tiger tail finished with a crimp.

Twisted Wire

Twisted wire can be used in combination with beads and semi-precious stone chips to create ethereal floral designs. It is best to use very thin wire (34-gauge craft wire). The brass and gold-finish wire is more attractive than the base-metal or grayed finish.

Allow about 5" of untwisted wire for each "frond" in your design. Thread on the bead or chip so that it is positioned in the middle of the length of wire. Then double up the wire; see Diagram HHH.

Starting near the chip or bead, twist the wire evenly until the bead or chip is secure; see Diagram III. Because the surfaces of semi-precious chips are uneven, there will be some movement of the chip at the end of the front; this is unavoidable, but it should not concern you. Movement often adds life to the design, and as long as the chip is in no danger of falling off, it will not be a detriment to the look of the finished piece.

Arrange the individual fronds as you like, then twist them together in groups to form flowers or leaf sprays.

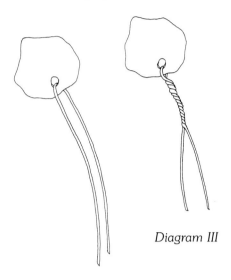

Diagram III

Diagram HHH

Endless Ear Hoops

Endless ear hoops can easily be decorated with beads. Choose beads with good-size holes; the gauge of the wire used in hoops is on the large side for strength, so some beads will not fit.

The hoops are sold in perfectly circular shape. You may have to relax the curve a bit by stretching out the circle in order to get long beads to fit over the curved wire. Simply bend the wire back into shape when the bead is in place. Finish the hoops by bending both ends as shown in Diagram JJJ.

Bend both ends.

Diagram JJJ

Endless Loops

The Endless Loop necklace is a continuous string of beads strung and tied into a joined loop; see Diagram KKK. Although no clasp is needed to wear this necklace, it is one of the most versatile basic designs you can make because there are numerous wearing options.

Cut the stringing fiber about 6" longer than the desired length of the necklace. Remember that the finished necklace must be larger than your head; a good length is 38" (see Five Strands Twisted Necklace, page 48).

String the beads in the desired order, then tie a square knot in the ends, being careful to take up all the slack before tightening the knot. Dab some glue on the knot and on the ½" of excess thread closest to the knot.

Run the thread ends back through the beads on either side of the knot so that approximately 1" of fiber is buried. Clip the excess.

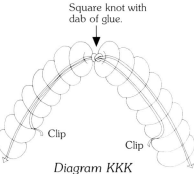

Diagram KKK

Double Loops

A good technique for stringing heavy beads with small holes is the double-loop method. Diagram LLL shows the path of the thread twice through one strand of beads. The strand is finished by tying a square knot in the two ends of the thread (after taking up all the slack in the thread) and burying the excess ends in the strand. Dab the knot with glue prior to burying the excess thread. Clip ends close to the beads. It's a good idea to place the knot in a section of the necklace so it will fall near the back of the neck.

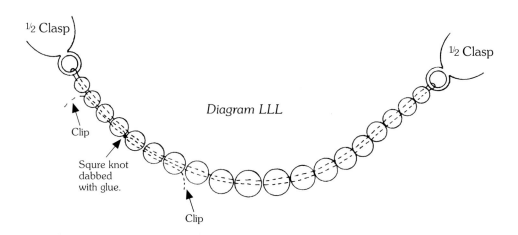

Diagram LLL

126

METRIC EQUIVALENCY CHART

MM-Millimetres   CM-Centimetres

INCHES TO MILLIMETRES AND CENTIMETRES

INCHES	MM	CM	INCHES	CM	INCHES	CM
⅛	3	0.3	9	22.9	30	76.2
¼	6	0.6	10	25.4	31	78.7
⅜	10	1.0	11	27.9	32	81.3
½	13	1.3	12	30.5	33	83.8
⅝	16	1.6	13	33.0	34	86.4
¾	19	1.9	14	35.6	35	88.9
⅞	22	2.2	15	38.1	36	91.4
1	25	2.5	16	40.6	37	94.0
1¼	32	3.2	17	43.2	38	96.5
1½	38	3.8	18	45.7	39	99.1
1¾	44	4.4	19	48.3	40	101.6
2	51	5.1	20	50.8	41	104.1
2½	64	6.4	21	53.3	42	106.7
3	76	7.6	22	55.9	43	109.2
3½	89	8.9	23	58.4	44	111.8
4	102	10.2	24	61.0	45	114.3
4½	114	11.4	25	63.5	46	116.8
5	127	12.7	26	66.0	47	119.4
6	152	15.2	27	68.6	48	121.9
7	178	17.8	28	71.1	49	124.5
8	203	20.3	29	73.7	50	127.0

YARDS TO METRES

YARDS	METRES	YARDS	METRES	YARDS	METRES	YARDS	METRES	YARDS	METRES
⅛	0.11	2⅛	1.94	4⅛	3.77	6⅛	5.60	8⅛	7.43
¼	0.23	2¼	2.06	4¼	3.89	6¼	5.72	8¼	7.54
⅜	0.34	2⅜	2.17	4⅜	4.00	6⅜	5.83	8⅜	7.66
½	0.46	2½	2.29	4½	4.11	6½	5.94	8½	7.77
⅝	0.57	2⅝	2.40	4⅝	4.23	6⅝	6.06	8⅝	7.89
¾	0.69	2¾	2.51	4¾	4.34	6¾	6.17	8¾	8.00
⅞	0.80	2⅞	2.63	4⅞	4.46	6⅞	6.29	8⅞	8.12
1	0.91	3	2.74	5	4.57	7	6.40	9	8.23
1⅛	1.03	3⅛	2.86	5⅛	4.69	7⅛	6.52	9⅛	8.34
1¼	1.14	3¼	2.97	5¼	4.80	7¼	6.63	9¼	8.46
1⅜	1.26	3⅜	3.09	5⅜	4.91	7⅜	6.74	9⅜	8.57
1½	1.37	3½	3.20	5½	5.03	7½	6.86	9½	8.69
1⅝	1.49	3⅝	3.31	5⅝	5.14	7⅝	6.97	9⅝	8.80
1¾	1.60	3¾	3.43	5¾	5.26	7¾	7.09	9¾	8.92
1⅞	1.71	3⅞	3.54	5⅞	5.37	7⅞	7.20	9⅞	9.03
2	1.83	4	3.66	6	5.49	8	7.32	10	9.14

Index

For information about supplies, please send a stamped self-addressed envelope to:

Ann Benson
P.O. Box 850
Amherst, Massachusetts 01004-0850